Back to the Front

First published by Jacana Media Pty (Ltd) in 2023

10 Orange Street
Sunnyside
Auckland Park 2092
South Africa
+2711 628 3200
www.jacana.co.za

© Leon Levy, 2023
© Cover image: Leon and Lilian Ngoyi, jubilant after being acquitted of treason.

All rights reserved.

ISBN 978-1-4314-3397-1

Cover design by Aimèe Armstrong and Maggie Davey
Editing by Colin Bundy
Proofreading by Lara Jacob
Set in Ehrhardt MT Std 12/16pt
Printed by Inside Data
Job no. 004064

Every effort has been made to identify copyright holders and obtain their permission for the use of copyright material.

See a complete list of Jacana titles at www.jacana.co.za

Back to the Front

A Memoir

Leon Levy

This book is dedicated to all activists, political and trade union leaders and anti-apartheid supporters who worked tirelessly for democratic change and the abolition of racism. They will always be remembered for their bravery, valuable inspiration, zeal and unstinting sacrifices.

Contents

Acknowledgements	ix
Preface	1
1 Childhood and Family Life	7
2 School – and the Wider World	23
3 Survivors, Jew Baiters and the Search for Solutions	37
4 A Decade of Growth and Change	47
5 My Vocation as a Trade Unionist	71
6 My Apprenticeship: Learning on the Factory Floor	89
7 A Historic Moment and New Trajectory	107
8 Building SACTU	127
9 On Trial for High Treason	151
10 Celebrations, Detention and Exile	179
11 Back to the Front	195
12 Taking on a New Role	211
Notes	227
Index	229

Acknowledgements

So many relatives, friends and close colleagues have consistently asked me to write about my role and experiences in active resistance to racism, apartheid and economic and political inequality. I have specifically acknowledged this in my preface.

This book would not have been possible to undertake without the support and huge interest of my family and particularly my wife Lorna Levy. Her support has been a major source of encouragement and indeed her assistance in selecting appropriate photographs for this book has been hugely helpful.

Special appreciation, acknowledgement and enthusiasm for my editor Colin Bundy is essential. His thirst for explanation, information and additional detail has been consistent and immensely helpful. I especially appreciated his knowledge and familiarity with the depth of the resistance to apartheid and the issues and people who I have written about. His patience and interest spurred my output while always taking pains to persuade me to fully share my experiences.

Preface

Why do I think, if I were to write my memoirs, it would be of any more use than those already published – except for Jonny and Daisy, my two grandchildren, and perhaps their parents, Emma and Mark, who have heard so much talk about the "struggle" years? Jonny, now almost 17 years old, is already tasked with school projects on personalities and policies of the former Nationalist government and the resistance to its unjust apartheid laws. Such laws as the spatial segregation of communities according to their racial origins (the Group Areas Act); Bantu Education, which provided limited and inferior education for African children; and the iniquitous pass system which controlled the movement of black people and dictated where they should live and work. So, there is, to a large degree, considerable information readily available. There is, therefore, seemingly little need to repeat what others have already written, with skill, passion and accuracy. Moreover, nowadays, in contrast to only a relatively short while ago, there are available a variety of digital innovations such as Google and YouTube,

"History on Line" and other sources which can be referred to for instant information.

But, as the years slip away, the argument for another veteran memoir is compelling. There are now a dwindling number of eyewitnesses who can say: I was in Kliptown where and when the Freedom Charter was adopted; I was Accused No. 4 in the 1956 Treason Trial; and I participated in events in the fifties and sixties, which inevitably led to police arrest, solitary confinement and, for some, torture in prison cells. In those times, I served on the district committee of the Communist Party, the National Executive Committee of the South African Congress of Trade Unions (SACTU) and the Congress Alliance committee, which led the campaign for the Congress of the People. I served on the committee that subsequently managed the programme of activities for the implementation of the Freedom Charter. In light of this, argument for another veteran autobiography may be more persuasive. More than that, there is a view that nearly three decades after the fall of apartheid it is time to assess whether post-liberation core beliefs and standards have altered or modified – and if so, why? I believe that now is the appropriate opportunity; and there are everywhere many "born free" young men and women who are eager to talk about what we did in those difficult years. They are asking whether aspirations have matched achievements and if expectations and values have changed or are now often interpreted differently. I can contribute to this discussion. We experienced dark and dangerous days during the unjust and oppressive rule of apartheid – when our cause was right against wrong – and wrong was literally a call to arms.

Apartheid's abuse of human rights has been eliminated, but do post-liberation innovations sufficiently match our expectations? As is the case with so many others of my generation, I have footprints in the past as well as the present. And there are so many who are assessing their impact and seeking solutions for the future. Now, as I think about the scope for more discussion on the struggle years, and new and different generational interpretations, I am persuaded there is merit in sharing my experiences and observations. It is important to join up the dots to understand and assess work in progress and our efforts to continue building a strong South African democracy. Thus, with much trepidation and respect for those who have shared their hopes and dreams with us, what follows are the facts of my life and the principles that inspired me.

Although I spent 34 years in exile, this book does not cover that period. The bulk of what follows deals with my life before I left South Africa in 1963. It chronicles my early life, my family background, and my entry into and experience of political activism. It recounts in some detail my involvement in trade union struggles in the 1950s, and especially in SACTU. It also describes how such activism came to be proscribed or at best curtailed by the security apparatus of the apartheid government. It tells of constant police surveillance, banning orders, detention without trial, and especially my being charged with high treason in a court case that impacted directly on my life for over four years.

The final two chapters narrate the years that began in July 1997 when Lorna, my wife, and I returned to South Africa: a journey not only to the land of my birth, but also back to the front of labour relations and human rights that had been the focus of my political life prior to exile. I resumed a role – as best I could – as an active participant in shaping the lives and aspirations of working-class people. The context was of course very different. In 1997, Nelson Mandela's government had been in power for just over three years and had enacted progressive industrial relations legislation while the Congress of South African Trade Unions (COSATU) was a member of the tripartite alliance with the African National Congress and the South African Communist Party. I was able to draw upon my extensive experience of industrial relations work while living in England and to apply it to post-apartheid South Africa. I worked initially for a leading labour consultant but moved to a post as a full-time commissioner in the new Commission for Conciliation, Mediation and Arbitration (CCMA).

I have chosen to focus on my South African years, in two periods which book-end my life in exile. Lorna has written a fine and fairly detailed account of the 34 years we lived in England, in her *Radical Engagements*, a well-received memoir. Instead of writing at comparable length about the years I lived and worked in England, the barest summary must serve to indicate how my understanding and experience of industrial relations were deepened and extended. I provide this at the beginning of Chapter 11. At very short notice, I was granted an exit visa by the security police in July 1963 – I was to be released from prison on condition that I left South Africa immediately and permanently. I arrived at Heathrow (as I wrote for the *Guardian* a few months later) "under the strangest circumstances, unwashed, dishevelled and completely bewildered by an atmosphere of freedom".[1] I was fortunate to be awarded a scholarship to study politics, economics and industrial relations at Ruskin College, Oxford, and for the next two years divided my time between London and Oxford.

The Oxford course provided me with crucial theoretical tools for work in industrial relations at a time when these were undergoing profound change in Britain. I worked for a time as a researcher for the Amalgamated Union of Engineering Workers before I spent three decades of work in a series of jobs for Mobil Oil, and then the Rootes Motor Company, which was bought out and became part of the Chrysler Motor Corporation. The 1970s, in particular, was a fraught period in British industrial democracy, punctuated with frequent strikes – and few sectors were more strike-prone that the motor industry to which I had gravitated as an industrial relations specialist. Chrysler was gripped by strikes and disputes at its different plants in Coventry, Glasgow and Dunstable. Lorna recalls that I "was always going somewhere, often to consult with Jack Jones and Hugh Scanlon, the 'kings' of the trade-union movement, to try to bring the workforce back to work".[2] Both the theory and practice of industrial relations, which I encountered in Britain, and the experience and skills I developed, were valuable assets during my 20 years with the CCMA. By then, I had returned to the front, to the land of my birth, and to an excitingly new South Africa.

One
Childhood and Family Life

My twin brother, Norman, and I were born at my parents' home on 7 August 1929 in Saxonwold, Johannesburg and I lived there until the age of four. I was the older twin – but only four minutes older! As is often the case with identical twins, Norman and I were extremely close to each other, right through childhood and into adulthood. He described us as "alike as two peas in a pod ... similar in dress, interests and attitudes", adding that "we almost always discussed everything we did and felt strongly about".[3] I summed up our relationship to a correspondent by saying that "the word 'we' was used a lot".

The family house was a stone's throw away from the Johannesburg Zoo and it was part of the morning routine to visit the animals. I think I learned to know the exact spot where each of the animals lived but remember best being lifted on to a saddle that was spread over an elephant's back. It was part of its training to carry visitors, mainly at weekends. I do not remember much about our house but recall the front garden and quite a lot of space for playing at the back. The house was named "Marigold" – a combination of my mother's name, Mary, and my sister's, Goldie. There was a sitting room furnished with brocaded purple curtains to match armchairs, and a settee. But what I recall most vividly was listening to the wireless and especially the BBC's Aunt Margaret's programme for children: memorably, on the occasion of our birthday once we twins were wished a happy day. We never lived in such a house again or enjoyed such a cosy routine.

My parents both came from Lithuania. My mother was born Mary Witten and lived in a village called Krekenava. She followed her father to South Africa in 1908, aged 12 – and for the rest of her life retained vivid memories of the village and her home, near the synagogue. I remember her account of the coal fires in the house and her grandparents sewing clothes for her, and from her stories of daily life she seems to have been happy there and clearly grew up in a family that was not desperately poor. Her memories of her childhood gave me an interest in sharing the places she had talked about, and when in 1993 Lorna and I visited Krekenava I was able to make various connections between the village and her reminiscences of it.

My father, Mark Levy, was born in 1891 in Weeds, a village near Minsk, that was then still in Lithuania. I understand that he moved to South Africa as a child with his father. I hardly knew him. I remember him being at home, ill in bed, and Norman and I standing at his bedside. I recollect him filling sweets into two cone-shaped paper serviettes and presenting them to us. However, I cannot remember what he talked about or precisely what he looked like. There is a blurred recollection that David, my elder brother, who was three years older than me, resembled him. David died in 2017 at the age of 93, where he lived in Australia with his family. Goldie and her family lived in Johannesburg. She passed away at the age of 78 in the year 2000. Her children, Marilyn and Colin now live in the USA with their families. Norman lived in Cape Town but his children Deborah, Simon and Jessica live in London. Sadly, Norman died on the 2 July 2021 after a short onset of lung cancer. Before he became an invalid my father ran a business: Levy's Provisions and Fishery. It was established in the 1920s, and I gather, from what was said, relatively well known. It was strategically positioned in President Street, not far from the Johannesburg City Hall.

The family left Marigold in 1933. I do not know why we did so, but can only speculate that the move may have been for financial or health reasons – or a combination of these. Whatever the case, we moved to a boarding house in Berea, Johannesburg, with the unlikely name of "Hollywood". Inevitably, I muddled it with the real thing. Norman and I shared a room with my parents. I assume Goldie occupied another room. David was already at boarding school at Marist Brothers College, which was, at that time, in the vicinity of Joubert Park in Johannesburg. He must have been about seven or eight years old. Norman and I were enrolled at the nearby kindergarten at the Berea Synagogue but I remember little else about it, apart from small chairs and tables – pink and blue.

In September 1935, we moved from Hollywood into a house in Loch Avenue, Parktown, a suburb of Johannesburg. On Sunday the 22nd of that month my father suffered a heart attack and died. My mother, aged 39, remained grief stricken for many years and faithfully visited his grave on Sundays. She kept his memory alive by talking about him and whatever recollection I have is coloured by what she related. She had to cope with her personal bereavement and loss of a mentor and enlightened partner. Her relationship with him was close. I gathered, from what she told me through the years, that he discussed much about life, literature and ideals with her. She spoke quite often of how they had enjoyed many picnics and social activities with friends.

Mother had a taste for classical music, although I do not recall her going to concerts. Those of her friends whom I remember – Annie Kotkin, Lilly Evans, Ray Segal, Rose Coblentz and Mrs. Forman – enjoyed interesting and compatible conversations. She also liked to play card games, especially Klaverjas and Rummy. I remember Mother's wry sense of humour and amusing thoughts. Her love for her children was unconditional and I think we all regarded her as an old and memorable soldier. There was something unmistakably heroic about the way she carried our family – financially, practically and emotionally – in her widowhood. My father's death left her as a widow now solely responsible for four children: Goldie was 13, David nine, and Norman and I had turned six a month before Father died. Mother kept the family together with an affection and determination which defied reality.

We grew up to understand the burdens of making ends meet and ensuring a roof over our heads, even if it meant moving house often, something like 14 times, between the years 1935 and 1956. An important observation regarding the dynamics of the family is the absence of animosity, envy and dissatisfaction among the siblings – or with our mother. We came to expect her midnight panic attacks and cries of "why me; what have I done to deserve this". Rather than talk, we listened. I doubt if we could have coped with such despair differently. Later and particularly in exile, in England, I could draw on the experience of late-night anguish and react more positively. The thing to do was to switch on the kettle, make tea, stay calm and respond with sincerity. The process was soothing and before night became day, we would go back to sleep and not mention it again. Thinking back to those times, I believe that they helped to stiffen reaction to crisis situations and assisted the development of leadership skills.

Reflecting on my early years, I think my childhood and early years of growth and development were unlike those of most of the local children of our age. We four children had to grow up quickly and learn to fend and think for ourselves. We did not eat together as a family; our home included a floating population of paying guests; and we had to find a corner to do our homework. Our recreation was limited. We enjoyed a few picnics but relatively little else; we visited few friends. Norman and I did, however, discuss political issues and the books we read while still quite young. In various ways we did not grow up in the ordered environment in which we imagined our peers lived.

Beyond any doubt, our family circumstances – and my mother's response to them – played an important part in shaping my life. By the time I turned ten years old, the family had moved house four times. Father had passed away; the Second World War had begun, and Mother had new and daunting responsibilities. Hardly a year after my father died, the family moved to a residential hotel. It was situated on Louis Botha Avenue, which was a rather busy Johannesburg highway, in the suburb of Berea. I remember how dangerous it was for young children to cross the busy road, and indeed there were one or two near misses when trying to do so. I cannot recall much about the "Villa Georgette" as was its name. Our family occupied two rooms that faced the highway. Anyway, it was only for a short time. We soon moved to an apartment in Bonvista Mansions in Hillbrow. It had two bedrooms, a dining room, a sitting room, and a rather large balcony, facing busy Twist Street, which incidentally led into the Louis Botha Avenue highway. The balcony was our space: it was here that we played with our toys and marbles. The furniture, which I assume Mother brought from the house in Parktown, comprised some rather elegant bookcases and a piano that travelled with us to other homes we moved to. I have some vivid memories of living in that block of flats: I am not quite sure which floor we lived on – possibly the second or third – but the fascination was the shiny wooden staircase banister. I remember Walter, the son of the owner of the building, and myself, sitting on the structure and sliding down faster and faster to the ground floor. The speed at which I travelled is particularly poignant now, looking back from my early nineties and finding myself, almost unbelievably, in old age.

I got to know some of the kids across the road, in Van Der Merwe Street, who played on the pavement until dusk. They invited me to play kennetjie, the Afrikaans word for a boys' game in which a short stick is flipped into the air by a longer stick, batted and hopefully caught by "fielders". It was like an impromptu form of baseball. Unfortunately, I have forgotten the names of most of those playmates, but I do remember the Israelstam brothers, Dan and his much younger brother Gerry. That was a friendship that lasted a long time as Dan became active in the political movement and Gerry and Sally Kowalski (his wife) supported the cause. From time to time I have flashes of memory of different aspects of our stay in Hillbrow, especially walking up Van Der Merwe Street to feed a kitten, which was owned by a lady who lived in Van Der Merwe Court. I remember my sister Goldie, who was then 18 years old and quite a good pianist and entertained us. She was awarded a silver medal at an Eisteddfod for her performance of Liszt's *Lebensraum*. She had many friends and livened up our flat with parties. She had a lot of friends, mainly from Habonim, who were now grown up and either studying or already working. It was swing time and jitterbug had given way to jive. Goldie and her friends took their turn in strumming out the latest songs and everybody danced or jived to the latest tunes. Like most kids, I messed around on the dance floor, when I should really have been tucked in bed. Despite the time lag, I do however remember the enjoyment, the atmosphere and the music, and it makes me smile.

But it wasn't fun all the time. I remember Mother leaving for business, early in the morning and returning home, after six o'clock or later in the evening, tired but uncomplaining. She had no one to lean on. She was father, mother and head of the family – and weary or not, she often read bedtime stories. She had domestic help, who also took and fetched us, the twins, to and from school. Sometimes, she invited a German Jewish refugee to stay with us. This, she felt, was the only practical thing she could offer, to support those ill-fated people, who escaped Hitler's unimaginable cruelty, with only their lives. My father had always hoped to bring members of his own family from Eastern Europe to South Africa and my mother honoured this wish after his death. It was 1937 or 1938 and my father's relatives must have been among the last of the Jewish emigrés able to leave Lithuania for South Africa. When the group arrived in Johannesburg, they included my father's brother and sister.

She decided to continue with the fish and groceries business that my father had founded. However, given the difficult financial situation in the country and the world, it was now both a difficult economic and physical struggle to maintain it. These were problematic times and although Mother possessed inner strength and determination the 1929 depression inevitably brought its social and economic consequences into family life. There was much confusion and political wrangling in the country, particularly regarding adherence to the Gold Standard. The effect on prices and trade impacted on the profitability of the family business; and holding on to it required essentially astute decision-making, training and administrative expertise. The staff required guidance and supervision. It was a time of uncertainty and social and economic depression. Mother required the proverbial wisdom of Solomon to constantly make wise and workable decisions. She tried hard from early morning until late but circumstances and the need for meaningful and useful advice were inhibiting factors. Nevertheless, there is much evidence to show she was determined to keep the family together, and soldier on. But circumstances eventually led to her selling the business a few years later.

I have no knowledge of the financial advantages or profit gained from the sale of the business, but she managed to obtain sufficient capital to finance her next endeavour: a trousseau, linen and lingerie boutique! It was what she wanted – a significant change from the setting in which she had previously become familiar: a different environment from a fish and grocery business that catered for daily provisions which customers must of necessity buy. She wanted a change to an environment where the pace was slower and the atmosphere conducive to selling, gowns, blouses and underwear. She imported them from Indo-China (Vietnam, Cambodia and other countries which at that time were colonies of the French empire). This was hugely different from what was familiar but for now she needed something rather different. When I reflect on what it involved, I am surprised by her courage in committing to a sphere in which she knew so little. She needed to acquaint herself with the role of shipping agents and gather experience in ordering sufficient stock for a clientele not yet established. There were basic customs and excise requirements which included an aptitude for accurate planning of credit facilities to maintain a steady flow of stock at prices her customers could afford. She had to understand risky fluctuating currencies, which often changed overnight. But she did manage to establish the business, "Mrs. M. Levy, Trousseau, Linen and Lingerie specialist", and began to build a clientele.

At first, she established a showroom at Greatermans Building, which was situated not too far away from the premises of the fish and grocery business. But soon she moved to a location with more scope for passing trade, and found what she was looking for, a few blocks away from Johannesburg's prestigious Wanderers football grounds. I visited the shop often by tram. It moved, at a pace, down the hill, from Twist Street past Joubert Park and turned right into Plein Street. Sometimes, Mother would send me on errands to fetch or carry various items or deposit money at the Netherlands bank (as it was then known). I remember visiting the shop with Ronnie Press – a friend who became a political activist – and sat in my usual spot, talked, and nibbled sandwiches. At that time, Ronnie and I were both about 11 years old. Who was to know that sometime later, when we were in our twenties, we would both be arrested and charged with high treason? But for now, it was 1940, and the world was witnessing the "Phoney War"– the lull before the terrible storm.

Mother persevered with the lingerie business, but Norman needed to rest at home for some months. This was to recover from the effects of a heart condition. Our doctor, Max Joffe, recommended this, as a necessary precaution, which turned out to be medically sound: Norman recovered after some time and the Levy twins went on to celebrate their 90th birthday on 7 August 2019! Mother regarded the need to nurse him at home a priority, and felt impelled to close the lingerie business, and find a way of attending to him. She was a practical and imaginative person and resolved to combine being at home with making a living. She decided to open a boarding house and rent a suitable place, which she found at number 3 Soper Road. This had previously been one of many of the boarding houses or hotels in Berea. Number 3 Soper Road had about 13 rooms, a large kitchen, dining room and lounge. The telephone, for use by the residents, was attached to a wall in one of the passages. The house was located within walking distance of shops in Kotze Street, where there was adequate public transport. It was a double-storey house, with no garden or much space at the back, except for rooms for waiters and cleaning staff. What was more, it was also occupied by a large black cat, who we named Felix. At the front of the house, there was a dark green hedge, which was a softer alternative to a conventional fence. As far as I can remember, the building was in reasonable condition. The project, of course, required capital and operational resources. I never asked how she put all her financial requirements together to establish the boarding house at number 3 Soper Road. It is reasonable to assume she may have had some of her own funds and some help from the bank and her friends. There were many of them who built up successful businesses in the twenties and thirties when she and my father were members of the Yiddish Cultural Federation.

Mother fitted out 13 rooms with suitable furniture: beds, wardrobes, side tables, wash basins, curtains and blinds. The latter had to be appropriate to shut out the light in the event of a "black out". This was an official precaution, required during the war in the event of an air-raid. There were members of the ARP (Air Raid Precaution) who patrolled the streets during air raid practices. It was a routine event that became less frequent as the prospect of an invasion by the enemy – Germany, Italy and later Japan – reduced substantially. Additional expenditure was required for furniture for bed-linen, towels and bedspreads. The lounge was furnished with some of the sitting room furniture, from our apartment in Bonvista Mansions, together with the rather important looking but familiar bookcases and our piano. In the dining room, there were at least 13 tables and an appropriate number of dining room chairs, white tablecloths, napkins and cutlery. The kitchen was a reasonable size with a scullery, and ample place for pots and pans of various sizes, as well as other necessary pieces of equipment.

We took it for granted that our 45-year-old mother knew the ropes. She had only herself to rely on, but the waiters were experienced and brought with them their special skills which helped her enormously. They wore white uniforms but Francis, a professional of long years standing, who was head waiter, sported a red sash. He was an immigrant from Malawi (which at the time was Nyasaland) and may not have had documents to live and work in the country; indeed, all of the three waiters may have been undocumented immigrants, but this was not a concern which worried Mother. I remember the rather elegant way the waiters prepared breakfasts, especially fruit: oranges and melons which they had a knack of peeling and cutting with small serrated knives. They brought with them the expertise of arranging tables and folding napkins attractively. Mother was general manager, supervisor, receptionist and cook. She planned the meals and wrote the menus by hand. She handled the accounts, but I think there were many administrative details which resided, mainly, in her head. Her priority was the management of the kitchen, the cooking and the menus.

Boarders were allotted tables but none were fixed specifically for the family. Goldie, Norman and I did not always eat our meals at the same time. We sat at available tables and were served in the same way as the boarders. Consequently, there was not much occasion for discussion, on what was happening at school or personal matters, concerning the family – only general conversation. We shared bedrooms but the patterns of sleeping arrangements changed frequently, depending on the need to create room space for boarders. This was the case throughout the years, wherever we lived and took in boarders. We made up secret nicknames for some of the boarders like "charging Bertha". She must have been about 70 years old and would stand or sit as near to the dining room as she could, waiting for the sound of the gong, which signalled that the dining room was open. She would "charge" at speed to her table and claim the attention of the waiters. There was the family with a couple of kids, whose father was a soldier but seemed to be available for all the meals. Mother coined the name "chocolate soldier". Then there was Mrs. K who was a Hebrew teacher. She became "the lady with the screaming kids": when she went out at night, the kids (who were three and five years old) shrieked until we pacified them. There was, of course, Miss A. She had large eyes, but one was bigger than the other; I think either I or Norman or the waiters nicknamed her "Big Eye".

After about two years, in early 1941, the boarding house, at number 3 Soper Road, kept afloat, but became too small to cope with the demand for accommodation. Mother found a larger house at number 21 Soper Road. This double-storey house was larger and came with 22 bedrooms which included a single-storey annex. There was a lounge, large kitchen, scullery and dining room. While there was not an established garden, there was a lawn, which I took upon myself to water and keep green. This, of course, provided me with the opportunity to spray water on some of the resident kids! The boarding house was named Agol House. This was a gesture of thanks to my mother's first cousin, Ann Goldstein, who provided the capital required for the new venture. She was a kind of fairy godmother. I recall her treating us (the twins) from the age of nine to 14, to Greatermans Stores, for an annual shopping spree. This was to celebrate Rosh Hashanah (Jewish new year) and the gifts included short trousers and as we grew older, blue suits and ties. Auntie Ann occasionally brought us piles of old comic strips, but we were too polite to tell her that we did not read them. Ann Goldstein died some years after I went into exile but I often think of her with much appreciation. The routines and arrangements at Agol House were much the same as before we moved from number 3 Soper Road. In August 1942 the twins turned 13 and although we were secular Jews, not at all religious but somewhat traditional, we followed the custom in this instance, as did my older brother David, of celebrating our Bar Mitzvahs at the Berea Synagogue, the venue of the kindergarten with the pink and blue chairs. That evening, my mother invited her friends to Agol House for a card party, for which, she used the dining room – and we were part of a dance party in the hall of Agol House. Goldie and friends played dance tunes on the old piano. Time moved on – and in 1943, when the war was still raging, Mother decided that it was time for her to make a change to something less strenuous. Agol House was closed, and Mother auctioned the furniture. We moved to number 12 Muller Street, Yeoville – a street just above the familiar busy highway, Louis Botha Avenue.

The Muller Street house comprised five or six bedrooms, some of which Mother used for a new venture! She and an old friend, Ray Segal, established a "cut, make and trim" operation. They invested in Singer sewing machines and employed three seamstresses. Mother took a course on cutting fabric for night dresses and ladies pajamas. They sold the garments to some of the department stores, such as Greatermans and John Orr. This was sometime in 1944. There was a market for this kind of sleep wear, especially because the war interrupted the import trade. Many clothing factories changed to produce army uniforms and related items such as helmets, hats and caps, boots shoes and canvas ware. The business eventually slowed down and stopped as the war was ending, and local and overseas manufacturers resumed their trade. So, after some short-term accommodation arrangements, Mother decided to rent a house at the corner of Grafton Road and Raleigh Street and take in a few boarders to supplement her income. One of the rooms she rented to the Communist Party. This served as an election room for Dr Percy Cohen, who was nominated as candidate to contest the election. It was not the first time that we accommodated the party at election time and the experience is memorable. There were many activists and leaders who we came to know well – and indeed work with – and whom we shared a political platform or indeed a prison cell or courtroom. This was the house which I remember best. We moved in when I was about 14 and developed the characteristics of an adult – and the political and social patterns of my life, my interests, friendships and a career path. It was also the house from which Goldie got married and David lived in when he began working as a pharmaceutical assistant. More than that, this was the house we lived in when the war with Germany and Japan ended.

Two

School – and the Wider World

Let me step back from the account of family circumstances and my mother's resolute efforts to bring up her young family in what I now realise were extremely challenging times, and resume my memoir with an account of my education and intellectual development more broadly.

I have a vivid recollection of the day I started at Observatory Boys' and Girls' school, in January 1936. As the school was situated at some distance from our apartment, on the corner of Twist and Van Der Merwe Streets, we travelled by tram, from Kotze Street in Hillbrow, to the Observatory tram terminus. On the first day of the term, the class teacher welcomed us, but was distracted by some giggling. She soon realised that the merriment stemmed from the sight of the identical twins, sitting next to each other, dressed in blue short trousers and yellow shirts. The official school uniform colours were white and grey – and our colourful outfits certainly did not conform with school regulations. Mother, surely, must have enquired about the dress code before she enrolled us. I assume, she did so when Goldie and David started at their schools. She was not an unusually eccentric person but could be unconventional.

The school was situated on a rather picturesque part of Observatory and surrounded by well-manicured lawns. I remember the pleasure of being taught to read and write, perched with pencil and slate, near the edge of the light-green grass. I enjoyed being asked to read aloud but cannot remember much of the content; but the class was well stocked with story books, and I had already developed a love of reading. Among other subjects we were taught our multiplication tables and some nature study. But these were elementary grades and, I imagine, age appropriate. Had it not been my first year at school, it would have been uneventful enough. In May that year, like millions of school children throughout the British Empire, we were presented with commemorative mugs, imprinted with the faces of King George V and Queen Mary. These marked the King's Silver Jubilee but, as is often the case in the course of history, it was not too long before the mugs would also mark the beginning of the end of Empire. Anyway, they were displayed, with other ornaments, on a shelf below our dining room ceiling, and followed us around for several moves.

By the time I reached standard 2 (or grade 3, as it is now known) the school authorities decided to change Observatory's status, as a co-educational school, to one for girls only. The boys were transferred to the Boys School, not too far away, at the edge of Bellevue, in the suburb of Yeoville. It was a red brick building, urban, and typically unattractive, unlike the leafy primary school down the road in Observatory. This was in 1938 and the seeds of Afrikaner nationalism were already rooted and attractive to Afrikaner nationalist teachers, who were developing their philosophy of Christian National Education and the reinforcement of the apartheid philosophy. But the main thrust of Afrikaner nationalism was not yet apparent and seemed at times to manifest itself mainly in anti-Semitic behavior. During the Second World War, while many English-speaking white South Africans joined the army, this meant that schools tended to be mainly staffed by racist teachers and likeminded anti-Semitic teachers. This scarcity of teachers, at that time, had a significant effect on the staffing of both primary and high schools that I attended.

Inevitably, the strains of economic hardship we were experiencing at home, the gloomy world outlook and other distractions, which interrupted total absorption in school and related activities, were factors that made school a less significant feature of my life. I think this, too, was the case with my siblings. What went on at school was seldom a feature of much discussion. Still, I developed a keen interest in history, although the scope for teaching this subject was limited (for political reasons) by the exclusion of major local and world events. The syllabus offered only a thin and one-sided view of the numerous colonial wars fought in the Eastern Cape, Zululand in Natal, and other parts of the country. There were too many contradictions involved in making sense of South African history – or making it interesting. Nevertheless, I found European history stimulating and liked it even more when I moved on to high school.

Athlone High School was situated in Bez Valley, which was not too far away from Observatory and Yeoville but required a tram ride to the terminus at Observatory and another short bus ride to the school. The school encouraged us to join clubs which met weekly – for chess, cooking and first aid among others, and a well-established debating society which I joined. Subjects of debate included the usual suspects, such as the pros and cons of capital punishment and argument for and against co-educational schools, as well as others that I have long since forgotten. Looking back, I did benefit from learning the techniques of arguing one's case. In the classroom, I studied Mathematics, including geometry and algebra, as well as Science, Afrikaans, French, English and History. The last two of these were my favourite subjects. I was taught English by a Mrs Greenberg, but I particularly wish I could remember the name of the history teacher whose lessons I enjoyed so much. Participation in the school cadet system was compulsory for boys, who were issued with khaki uniforms: short trousers and tunics. Rifle practice was truly a problem – as my aim was shocking – and it surely could have been a cause for concern, had it involved more than practice. I learned little about warfare and neither did I enjoy it.

Among the other pupils, I was friendly with George Bizos, Paul Berhaus, Beryl Gordon, Beattie Simons, Jack Glatskin and Ettie Zimmerman. I did not follow the fortunes of my schoolmates after leaving school, as one normally would. I seldom had the opportunity to do so and lived, increasingly, in different social and political worlds. This, of course, has much to do with the story of my life, which this memoir is all about. However, an important exception is George Bizos, who was in the same class at school as me. He went on to become an advocate who would play an important part in defending political activists against charges of treason and other political offences. George was part of the team which assisted our counsel in the preparation of defense material in the 1956 trial for high treason. He went on to distinguish himself in major political cases, and became a friend and important colleague of Nelson Mandela, throughout the 27 years of his life in prison and thereafter, until Mandela's death on 5 December 2013.

I left Athlone High at the end of Standard 8 (as it was then known), having turned 16 a few months earlier. I needed to earn money to contribute to the hard-pressed family set-up and entered full-time work (described in the following chapter). But I also enrolled in Damelin College, which was set up in 1943 by Benjamin (known as Bennie) Damelin to provide intensive part-time teaching evening classes. Bennie was quite a remarkable teacher, and I was able to matriculate with distinction in mercantile law. I also did well in the other subjects, English, Afrikaans, History, Botany and Commerce. Damelin provided me effectively with a rapid 'short cut' to matric even while I was working.

The world of books

Schooling may have constituted my formal education, but books and reading – and the privilege of growing up in a bookish home – were far more influential in broadening my mind, shaping my views, and ultimately in making me the young man I became. There were many influences from which my thoughts and beliefs originated. My sentiments, ideas and political actions were derived to a significant degree from what I saw around me. But reading, or being read to when I was young, contributed richly to my development. My mother was an avid reader. She had varied tastes and introduced me to many of the celebrated classics of British, French and Russian writers. There was much I read that shaped the direction of my political beliefs and human values, but it will suffice to recall some of the literary, cultural and philosophical works that interested and concerned me when I was growing up. Many of these books strengthened my resolve to resist significant compromises on principles which challenged right from wrong. Dickens' novels – especially *David Copperfield*, *Oliver Twist*, *Martin Chuzzlewit*, *Great Expectations* and *The Old Curiosity Shop* – were impressionable stories; about poverty, homelessness, treachery, fraud, hypocrisy, kidnapping and foul play. I was riveted by Dickens' description of the plight of people caught up in the troubles of debt, financial misfortune and inevitable penury in the poorhouses. I was moved by Gorky's novels, especially *Lower Depths*, which created an enduring observation of how poverty caused relationships to disintegrate. I read almost all the plays of Bernard Shaw and especially recall *Major Barbara*. These and many other plays and stories held my interest and imagination. They attracted my attention to ideas and organisations which could offer solutions, to assisting victims of circumstances that were not always of their making.

When I was very young, Mother read stories to me, among which were well-known Yiddish tales. She was a fan of Sholom Aleichem and other Jewish writers who wrote in Yiddish. My father left a library of impressively bound books, which were written by important Yiddish authors such as Sholom Asch, I.L. Peretz and Sholom Aleichem. Aleichem's adventures of Tevye the Milkman were favourites. Tevye was a milkman, who got into extraordinary scrapes. He was daring and dodgy and operated in shtetls (villages) in Lithuania. These stories inspired the musical *Fiddler on the Roof* and personified life in the shtetls. Underlying the humour and pathos, Aleichem was confronting the tensions and oppression of Jews in Tsarist

Russia. These stories prompted reminiscences, such as the much-feared pogroms against Jews and the fear created by Russian gendarmes, whom my Mother recalled, pressing their way into Jewish homes in search, among other things, of "army dodgers". This had to do with sons who had not presented themselves for Tsarist army service, as the Tsar's edict required. She recalled that Jews in the shtetl warned one and another of the presence of "Buttons", a clandestine reference to the shining buttons on the gendarmes' tunics. Anti-Semitism, and global antagonism towards Jewish people, have always been racist issues which worried me. This was a constant theme at Hashomer Hatza'ir, a Jewish youth movement, which I joined at an early age. It mattered to me to seek solutions to the problems of anti-Semitism and poverty.

The humanitarian role of Emile Zola and his powerful exposé of anti-Semitism evoked my interest and admiration. I was especially interested in the Dreyfus case. I admired Zola's tenacity in exposing the false accusations against Alfred Dreyfus, a Jewish general in the French army, who was a victim of anti-Semitism and falsely accused of spying. I did not read Zola's *J'Accuse*, but Mother talked about it. She admired the courage of Emile Zola and read and discussed many of his novels. At around the age of 15, I read Zola's masterpiece, *Germinal*. It was a story of hardship, obstinacy, love, greed and different shades of human behaviour. It was, for me, an insight into exploitation, in this case in the French mining industry. The novel centres on a particular coal mining town, Montsou, in the far north of France. Zola describes the anguish of the workers as they push their carts down the pit. He paints the picture of severe oppression and workers pressed to breaking point and eventually resorting to strike action which results in police and army intervention. I also read many of the novels in Honoré Balzac's *Human Comedy* and appreciated French realism of the period 1830 to the early 1890s. I read a lot – about life and people as they were; kind, cruel, rich, poor, miserly, generous, drunken, scheming, duplicitous, unfaithful, disloyal. This was the period when writers and artists wrote and painted as they saw life.

I discovered Greek tragedy and was fascinated by the dramas, especially Sophocles' *Oedipus Rex*. When I was about 20 years old, I auditioned for a part in Taube Kushlik's production of Oedipus and was accepted for the chorus. The production was well received, and continued for a few weeks. It was an interesting experience and I went on to read more Greek classical literature. I especially liked Sophocles' *Antigone*, and Aristophanes' comedy *The Frogs* and a few of Euripides' plays. I was also lucky to come across the bombastic and uncontainable vigour and energy of the Renaissance scholar Rabelais. I admired his Gargantuan criticism of French educationalists and pretentious officialdom. His satirical observations stayed with me and sharpened my critical faculties. After the end of the Second World War, there was considerable interest in the writings of Sartre. I was curious about his ideas on the role of the individual – as distinct from more determinist ideas, driven by changing effects of prevailing modes of production. His philosophy was interesting, and although I did not sustain or extend my interest, there was much to appreciate, especially on different themes, regarding an individual's full control over his or her will as distinct from the element of determination in collective behaviour. Later in life, engaged in mediation work,

I often recalled what Sartre had to say about an individual's ability to control his own will and impose it.

But my reading did not involve only fiction. I read quite widely about 20th-century history and the inter-war years, and especially about the Russian Revolution of October 1917. I was fascinated by John Reed's book *Ten Days That Shook the World*. This led me to novels, books and magazines about the Soviet Union, which deepened my interest. This, in turn, led me to study seriously the collective works of Karl Marx and Frederick Engels, and also works by Vladimir Lenin and Joseph Stalin. I read much of Mao Zedong's and Zhou Enlai's writings. I found Marx and Engels' *Das Kapital* a daunting experience, an overwhelming (but convincing) explanation of the capitalist system. I was intrigued by the logic in Engels' *Anti Duhring*, of the inevitable withering away of the state – when socialism is achieved and the coercive government of persons is replaced with the administration of things. Production, he envisaged, would be guided by administrators.

There continued to be much written about Russia and the Bolshevik Revolution, which dominated political life, ideological positions, beliefs and values. This was especially so in the war years, when Roosevelt, Churchill and Stalin commanded the scene as close allies, supposedly for a successful and happier future without wars. I continued reading widely about the international friction between the West and the East. At the age of 20, I lived in an impressionable environment, in an atmosphere in which post-war tensions were mounting, and the communist and capitalist worlds were increasingly engaged in a tug of war for economic and political allegiance. From that time to this, there has been a war, somewhere, in every continent in which the USA, British, Russian, Chinese, Middle Eastern and European influences were in the background. I chose socialism, both as a philosophy of life and a practical path to social economic and political upliftment. I believe that this would almost certainly have been so, even if the Cold War had not come about.

I was excited by Marx and Engels' rousing Communist Manifesto; especially the immortal words, "a Spectre is haunting Europe, the Spectre of Communism". This was written for a conference of the second Workers' International, in London in February 1848. It was the year in which revolutions were taking place in several countries in Europe and lasted until 1856. It was a definitive statement and explanation of the role of the existing class struggle and the nature and forms of future class warfare; notably the effect of constantly changing modes of production. I regarded the Manifesto as a way forward. It provided a sense of direction – a kind of certainty. It suggested confidence that our goal (of a just and economically fair and equitable society) was achievable. I used every opportunity to familiarise myself with "scientific socialism". I read in the quiet comfort of parks, such as the one near Harrow Road (now renamed Joe Slovo Drive). It is a long road which starts in the suburb of Yeoville and ends in Doornfontein. I read during my lunch hours, or whenever I had to wait, in long and slow-moving queues. I particularly recall Lenin's *Imperialism: The Highest Stage of Capitalism*. I was reminded of reading this, when some years later, a Special Branch detective casually remarked when I was released from 90-day detention, "You were always reading Lenin". Of course, I made no comment. But sometime later, my twin brother Norman told me that when he was in detention, a Special Branch detective mentioned the same thing about me to him.

Some years later, in the early 1950s, I decided to study further and enrolled, at Harvard College (not connected with Harvard University in the United States of America). The college was known in downtown Johannesburg for its Bachelor of Commerce courses, and I enrolled as a part-time student. I attended classes in the evenings in order to carry on working and contributing to the family income. I was an enthusiastic student but by then my eagerness for political and trade union activity demanded increasingly more of my time. Inevitably, I had to make the choice whether to carry on with the course and decided not to. I handed over the books which I had acquired for the course to a teenaged Thabo Mbeki, who almost a half a century later in 1999, succeeded Nelson Mandela as President of the new democratic Republic of South Africa. Some of the books I was using were of special interest to him, especially the works of the economist Richard G. Lipsey. Thabo proceeded to study economics at the University of Sussex.

For me, further studies had to wait, until I went into exile in 1963 – and was awarded a scholarship to Ruskin College, Oxford, in England. This was a major opportunity for me to add to the stock of knowledge about economics and politics that I had obtained through these years of intensive reading in private. At Ruskin, between 1964 and 1966, I read economics and political science, industrial relations and studies of developing countries. Economic theory, both micro and macro, were of enormous benefit and lasting importance. My studies required much preparatory reading and discussion. I particularly benefitted from bi-weekly tutorials, especially on Hobbes, Rousseau, John Stuart Mill, Burke, Descartes and more on Marx.

The world at war

Like so many of my generation around the world, I have a vivid memory of the day when Great Britain declared war on Germany. It was on 3 September 1939. We were seated around the radio in the sitting room of our flat in Bonvista Mansions in Hillbrow. King George VI broadcast the British government's declaration of war against Germany. I was ten years old, and too young to understand all that was said; but what I remember, so clearly, was the concern and fearfulness of my mother. It was, no doubt, the same for everyone who heard the news. I recall my mother's reaction. She worried about the stance of South Africa, especially whether the leaders of the Nationalist party would use the situation to ratchet up their hatred of Jews and their overt support for Hitler and the Nazi regime. She was referring to such leaders as D.F. Malan and Oswald Pirow (the latter, as it turned out 17 years later, was appointed chief prosecutor in the Treason Trial, in which I was Accused no. 4). The Afrikaner nationalist movement *Ossewa Brandwag* established an overtly Nazi storm trooper-type movement in the 1930s and was already causing riots. I grasped the picture of a dark cloud on the horizon, and recall writing a letter to my twin brother Norman who, at that time, was in hospital and diagnosed with scarlet fever. I told him, solemnly, that Britain was in a state of war with Germany. He too remembers this apocalyptic letter, of so many years ago. I also recall looking at *Ossewa Brandwag* posters in the streets, not far from where I lived. These raged about Jews and were replete with invective and threats about what was in store for them.

It was in 1940 in primary school that our class teacher, Miss Hayes, announced, with sadness, the fall of Paris – that was on 14 June when I was not yet 11 years old. We knew too, that there were some teachers who supported the National Party and were sympathetic to Hitler and Germany. There was, indeed, an incident when our Afrikaans language teacher commented to the class that Jews were mongrels. We reported this to our mother and she and other parents of Jewish children protested to the school head. I am glad we reacted to racist remarks and most importantly that we learned the value of standing up to racial prejudice.

I followed the course of the war closely and, as the years moved on slowly, I was troubled and impressionable. I heard about South African soldiers who were "killed in action" or had become prisoners of war in north Africa. There was concern that South Africa was vulnerable to invasion; we watched vivid pictures at the movies, showing victims of destruction as well as the heroism of people who were in resistance movements in occupied war-torn countries. We talked about the terrible persecution of Jewish men, women and children. News of the gassing of Jews in the concentration camps filtered through later. I read in the Johannesburg *Rand Daily Mail* about the sieges of Moscow and Leningrad and was delighted when they were broken by Russian armies and – as the tide turned – there were outstanding and daunting allied actions after the landings on the Normandy beaches in June 1944. In 1945, when I was 15 years old, I was enraptured when 20th Century Fox news showed Russian troops and tanks occupying Berlin. I remember standing in Raleigh Street, Yeoville, reading the *Rand Daily Mail*'s jubilant banner headline, which reported Germany's unconditional surrender. It was the end of the war in Europe, and I looked up to the sky and felt free. I kept that newspaper cutting for many years, together with other special news events. From that day to this, I have looked at the world as a whole and am moved and heartened by outstanding events.

Three
Survivors, Jew Baiters and the Search for Solutions

This chapter reflects upon my Jewish background and how it interacted with my broader social and political beliefs, as these took shape. Looking back, my Jewish identity did not really interest me as a young man. I became more aware of it, and more interested in it, upon my return to South Africa after three decades in exile. It merits a brief discussion here.

My parents, as I have indicated, were part of a significant influx of Jewish immigration, before and after the turn of the 20th century. "Waves of newcomers – the overwhelming majority from Lithuania – sought security and opportunity in South Africa" and after the discovery of gold "the center of Jewish life moved to the Witwatersrand".[4] By the time my parents set up home in Johannesburg they were among a Jewish population of over 25,000. By the time I was born, the suburbs of Hillbrow, Yeoville and Bellevue were home to large clusters of economically stable and culturally more assimilated

Jewish people than the poorer and culturally more orthodox and predominantly 'Litvak' Jewish population of southern suburbs like Ferreiratown. A study of Johannesburg's Jewish community has suggested that in the 1920s Jews responded to rising antisemitism by assimilating culturally (at least in language and dress) even while moving into close proximity with each other and creating areas with concentrations of Jewish families, creating spaces which were safe territories for the Jews of Johannesburg.[5] I think this characterises my parents; for all their enjoyment of Yiddish literature, they were not at all locked into Yiddish or Jewish religious identities. They were secular, and entirely at ease in English-speaking South Africa, as were their similarly acculturated Jewish friends and associates.

I do not know much about my father's interests or the extent of his political views, although the evidence suggests that he was a socialist. He and my mother were both associated with the Jewish Workers Club (and later my mother donated to it the family's entire collection of books written by Yiddish writers). My father was also the chairman of the South African committee, established in the late 1920s or early 1930s that supported the Birobidzhan project – a Soviet proposal for a Jewish homeland in the far east of Russia. Stalin's project saw the establishment in 1934, in the far east of Russia, of what was theoretically a home for Jews in the Soviet Union but turned out a profound failure. I do not know what Father knew about the initial phase of the "Jewish Autonomous Region" as it was created just the year before he died. He wrote poetry and admired the work of many Yiddish writers. Mother talked about his respect for her and what he taught her about life, ideals and meaningful practicalities. The Yiddish Cultural Federation, with its like-minded members of the Johannesburg Jewish community, seemed to be their niche. They developed friendships with people, whose names were, and still are familiar to me, as well known Jewish intellectual role-players. From what I can remember from my mother's reminiscences about their lifestyle, they enjoyed many picnics and social activities.

My mother may well have been influenced by his political views, certainly his thoughts on the Soviet Union. I recall her taking me to the Silver Hall, which was in the Commodore Hotel in Berea when I was about 11 years old. It was a political meeting, at which Hilda Watts spoke. Hilda was a prominent Communist Party activist and an orator of note (whom I later got to work with and know well).

It is an obvious point but an important one: my generation of Jewish men and woman and their children are all survivors of crimes against humanity and the grotesque practice of genocide. I was about 16 years old, in 1945, when the Nuremberg trials commenced, and the German perpetrators were charged with their dreadful crimes. In the case of the Jewish victims of the Holocaust, they were subjected to all of the 11 classifications of crimes against humanity which were codified, much later, in 1988. This was when the definition of crimes against humanity were incorporated in article 7 of the Rome Statute, of the International Criminal Court (ICC). These crimes were murder, extermination, enslavement, torture, forcible transfer of populations, imprisonment, rape, prosecution, enforced disappearance and, significant to note, apartheid. In 1945 South Africa did not yet have television, so we followed the course of the Nuremburg trials, as reported on the radio or in the newspapers, as closely as we could.

I was already a member of the Hashomer Hatza'ir, a left-wing Jewish youth movement, which I joined in 1941 when I was 12 years old. There was little information, at that time, of what was happening in the concentration camps, concerning the systematic extermination of deported and imprisoned Jewish and other groups of people who were deemed undesirable. But we talked about the evidence of the humiliation, deprivation, and physical and emotional persecution of Jews in Germany, from the time Hitler came to power. Many of the Hashomer members were first-generation Jews and some may have been born in Germany or Eastern Europe. An historian of the Jewish community in South Africa points out that Zionist youth movements – and especially Hashomer Hatza'ir – "provided a stimulus for political awareness and sometimes a training ground for radical activism, which were otherwise lacking in the adolescent experiences of most Jews".[6] He quotes Baruch Hirson, who was intensely involved in Hashomer Hatza'ir, and described it as "a crucible of political development".[7]

I was persuaded by Nathan Maister, a friend at Yeoville Boys School, to attend Hashomer meetings, which he said, were very different from what we were used to in Habonim, to which Goldie had introduced Norman and me. Habonim was a long-established Jewish Zionist movement (which was established in the United Kingdom in the 1920s) and was associated with the British Labour movement. There were, of course, discussions on the history and traditions in what, at that period, was called Palestine. But the style and content of the Hashomer Hatza'ir was very different. The meeting place was a vacant shop in a shopping centre in Johannesburg's Raleigh Street. The dress code was a statement of the movement's egalitarian socialist ideals. Boys wore blue shirts and trousers and girls wore similar blue tops and slacks or skirts. The use of lipstick and similar products was frowned upon. The emphasis was on the rejection of bourgeois class values and conventions, especially attitudes to material possessions and property, and the dress code was a metaphor to express this.

We sang revolutionary and folk songs and danced to the tunes of Hebrew songs, especially the Hora (a circle dance which originated in the Balkans). At times, we would have meetings at members' homes. I remember the blue-shirted chaverim (friends) meeting in the back yard of our Muller Street house. We danced the Hora and sang songs to the delight of my mother. She could hear the obvious merriment throughout the house. For me topics for discussion at meetings were interesting and appealing. We talked about religion (atheists and believers), religious observance, fasting on Yom Kippur, and the abuse of religion to suit selfish and exploitative class or group interests. This was all food for thought. What I did not immediately digest became clearer later and found expression or answers to which I did not fully appreciate at the time. We explored questions concerning sex and our responsibilities to ourselves as individuals, to society and to parental control. The membership shared a culture which was inclusive of relevant social and political issues of the day, and we were bonded by mutual appreciation of shared social and political values. Not surprisingly, it was difficult for an individual to opt out of the organisation and revisit the immediately accessible world of convention, commodities and, yes, responsibilities which concerned the individual and not the collective. This was not an easy break for anyone but certainly more difficult for women who returned to conventional dress codes, cosmetics and less demanding personal, political and social commitments.

However, at the centre of my concerns, was the search for a *solution* to end the persecution of Jews. The Hashomer Hatza'ir looked to the ideas and philosophical thoughts of Dov Ber Borochov – a theoretician and active campaigner. He visualised the creation of a bi-national state, consisting of Jews and Arabs in Zion. He was a Marxist Zionist, who was born in the Ukraine in 1881 and died in December 1917. He was prominent in the development of the Yiddish language and instrumental in 1891 in creating, in the Ukraine, the Zionist Socialist Workers Union. He opposed the idea of creating a Jewish homeland unless, he insisted, it was in Zion. There were at that time ongoing discussions on a homeland for Jewish people. There was much discussion on Uganda as a possibility, and also Stalin's offer of Birobidzhan on the Chinese Russian border.

Borochov's model of a bi-national state resonated with me, even though I was very young and did not concern myself with the theoretical arguments within his Marxist Socialist movement in the Ukraine. This was about whether intellectuals and academics sold their labour power on the labour market – on the same basis as the proletarianisation of Jewish workers. I suppose his ideas may have been revisionist. What interested me was his solution, a Jewish homeland, for what it seemed was for all who live in it. This did make sense to me and I supported it throughout my adolescent years. I liked the people who I met at, the study classes, the outdoor experience of meeting in Balfouria's leafy area of Johannesburg's Highland's North. I enjoyed the singing of songs, such as *Avanti Populo*, the Italian version of the Red Flag, songs of the Spanish civil war and those sung by the early *chalutzim* who had moved to Israel and were living in kibbutzim (collective agricultural communities).

This was a period of huge transformation and events moved quickly. Soon there would be the creation of the State of Israel. Many of the members of Hashomer Hatza'ir by this time had hopes or expectations of ultimately moving to the new Jewish homeland. Although I was under 18 and not involved in secret training, some older members of the Hashomer may have been involved in it. I gathered that training for the Hagenah (the main Zionist paramilitary organisation of the Jewish population in latter period of the British Palestine mandate) and Palmach, its elite fighting force. Palmach was founded in Palestine in 1941, and the older "Hashomerniks" proudly supported and sang songs about it. Sadly, one of our young South African leaders, Gideon Rosenberg, who rushed to Israel at the start of the Arab-Israeli War in 1948, was killed within the first few days of the conflict. His sister, Ruth, was also one of our leaders as were Dave Weinberg and Jack Halperin.

At that particular time, the Hashomer Hatza'ir was troubled about the creeping drift of fascism in South Africa. It was becoming increasingly rampant and violent. The Hashomer Hatza'ir attracted people like Joe Slovo and Baruch Hirson, who joined the "movement" and later became prominent and important leaders in the South African struggle against apartheid. The Hashomer leadership was in contact with the South African Communist Party and offered support, in resisting organised Nazi sympathisers who were bent on wrecking regular anti-fascist protest meetings which took place at the Johannesburg City Hall steps on Sunday nights. I attended some of those scary fracases. Although, I was not injured, I witnessed broken noses and teeth, and the blood of comrades who stood up to those thugs and Jew baiters. We suspected they were probably members of the police force dressed in plain clothes.

A question frequently put to me was what drew me, apparently so unconditionally, into active politics and trade unionism? It is a fair question. However, in South Africa, what is often meant by this question is: how and why was a white person caught up in the black people's struggle against racial, economic and social discrimination? There is no single, glib answer to the question. In my case, there were many reasons: these included the books I read which influenced and shaped my intellectual development and political views; the outbreak of the Second World War and its passage which preoccupied my early teenage years; the dreadful fate of so many Jews at the hands of the Nazis; and in South Africa the threat of the Afrikaner nationalist movements (Malan's National Party and the proto-fascist *Ossewa Brandwag*); and prejudice against Jewish people and hostile antisemitic activities. Moral values of my parents and siblings obviously played an intangible part alongside the external factors I have listed.

As this chapter suggests, my views and experiences were also shaped by being born into a Jewish family in a particular society at a particular time. Gideon Shimoni (who incidentally interviewed Norman and me during his research for a fine book) poses the question: how does one explain the disproportionate involvement and salience of persons of Jewish birth among whites involved in radical political opposition to the apartheid regime? He argues that those young Jewish adults who adopted left-wing politics were "doubly marginalized": they did not identify with established white society, nor did they identify with the established Jewish religious community. They then tended to associate socially and politically with other like-minded Jews. They found, he proposes, "a warmly embracing cosmopolitan home – a sense of belonging and dedication, social no less than political, that they could find neither in conventional white society nor in the sectarian Jewish community".[8] I suspect that this does apply in part to my own political trajectory, although to what degree is impossible to say. I would add an important caveat. What Shimoni's model rather leaves out is the extent to which my radicalisation was a direct reaction to the daily racism and the economic inequalities so prominent in South Arica. I know that when Norman and I reflected on our lives, he also emphasised the extent to which his political education included a visceral reaction against the everyday realities of white minority rule and black rightlessness.

Many decades after the events described in this chapter, in November 2015, I received an unexpected recognition from the South African Jewish Board of Deputies. The Board admitted that it had not done justice to Jewish members of the community who made sacrifices during the apartheid era. At a packed annual congress of the Board, I was presented with the Rabbi Cyril Harris and Ann Harris Human Rights Award to which I responded with an acceptance speech. The flattering text of the award honoured me "for a life spent in the pursuit of justice for your fellow South Africans and for the rights of the vulnerable and under-privileged in our society". It mentioned details of my career in the struggle and concluded: "You stand tall amongst those brave men and women of all races and creeds who took a stand against injustice, and whose vision and sacrifices made possible the birth of a free South Africa that truly belongs to all who live in it."

Four
A Decade of Growth and Change

In 1953, when I was 24 years old, I became a full-time trade unionist. It was a defining moment in my life story. It gave practical form to my political beliefs; it also determined the shape and scope of my life. It transpired that I would spend the next six decades and more working in trade unions, industrial relations and mediation. Subsequent chapters will describe my years organising South African workers but this chapter recounts my work experiences between my school years and 1953 as well as an account of my deepening political activism.

The world of work

I had some pleasant and sometimes entertaining work experiences in the commercial world before and after I left school. My first employment of any kind was in the form of school holiday jobs which provided a modest but useful income and valuable experience. These holiday jobs were mainly at Solly Kramer's liquor store and other retail shops in the centre of

Johannesburg. On one school end-of-term holiday, I and other friends got jobs with the Central News Agency (CNA). This entailed our writing the price on the inside cover of each of the vast range of books the company distributed to its network of stores and bookshops. Unfortunately, the job came to an abrupt end when the manager rushed into the large room where all the school kids were marking the books and demanded that we stop making a noise and cease the incessant chatter. One of the schoolboys started to argue the point and when he was fired on the spot, we all followed him out into the street. Needless to say, all 20 of the book price markers were dismissed and that was the end of my association with the CNA. This was an important experience for me. Firstly, it was an act of solidarity with a colleague who was speaking up for all of us who were responsible for the noise. And, secondly, it demonstrated how quickly an unimportant dispute could get out of control and how necessary it was to achieve strong leadership skills.

After I had left school at the age of 16, my first full-time job was with Bacher Aaron, a whole-sale clothing merchant. The company was situated in Market Street along with numerous others: large, small and in some cases prestigious long-established companies. The Bachers were well known and each of the brothers had their own business, not too far away from where I was, in Market Street, Johannesburg. Bacher Aaron imported much of its stock and catered for a large market in villages and towns throughout the country. I was responsible for selecting and supervising the dispatch of orders. Many of the company's customers had retail wholesale businesses in what was then known as South West Africa (now Namibia). One of my job requirements was to manage the exportation of the goods to that country. It required much preparation and quite detailed information for the local Customs and Excise Department's approval. This was a boon for me, as there were long queues at the customs office, which enabled me to spend much time reading, mostly Marx and Lenin. I particularly remember being totally engrossed in Lenin's thesis "Imperialism the highest stage of capitalism". I may already have been under observation by the Special Branch of the police who subsequently mentioned my choice of reading!

There were many useful experiences I enjoyed in this job. I realised that if you take your responsibilities seriously, whatever the environment or the job, there is much that adds to one's stock of skills and general knowledge. It is also worth mentioning that although the staff at Bacher Aaron was not unionised, I joined the National Union of Distributive Workers (NUDW). I attended a general meeting of the Johannesburg branch which took place at the Trades Hall. I participated in the discussions, asked questions, and was nominated and elected a committee member. This often happens in the trade union movement and probably elsewhere too! Long after I left Bacher Aaron and became a full-time trade unionist, I was detained during the 1960 state of emergency and the NUDW branch secretary sent me a solidarity gift of fifty pounds. My early NUDW experience was probably a stepping stone of sorts towards what became my vocation as a trade unionist.

After a couple of years with Bacher Aaron, my next job was better paying and an interesting opportunity to work in a manufacturing environment. Gummed Tapes was a fair-sized paper converting manufacturer. Its core products were glue-based adhesive paper, packaging tape and green waxed paper.

Also included in the product range were innovatively striped cake and candy boxes and a new and intricately designed, state-of-the-art cardboard container for eggs. All were an integral part of its major products. The company grew larger in succeeding years and was eventually sold long after I left in 1954. It was situated alongside the old (and no longer used) goldmines. The surrounding mine dumps were covered in dust and grime and were the subject of Johannesburg residents' wrath; the wind, relentlessly and indiscriminately, carried the dust into the homes of the posh and poor. My role was to be a administrator to the managing director, who held meetings of the Johannesburg sales team every morning at 8 o'clock. Each day the sales team submitted their order forms, detailing the items sold the previous day. My job was to scrutinise them and submit them for processing in the manufacturing area.

It was mandatory for the sales team to attend the daily meetings which were chaired by the managing director Mr Sydney Berman. The meetings were held in his rather well-furnished office. Sydney would ask me to present the details of the orders and especially the range of products sold the previous day. It was not always a happy moment for those representatives who had an unsuccessful sales performance the previous day, especially when they were asked difficult questions. The objective of these meetings, however, was to enthuse the sales staff with the importance of the product, its quality and why it was superior to that of the company's competitors. The representatives were expected to be passionate about the product when describing its virtues to customers. Sydney would demonstrate how this was to be done. He would choose one of the new lines: a candy-striped cake box or a roll of green waxed paper, or a new range of packaging tape, and with considerable emotion, speak to each feature of the product's uniqueness. Whether or not these tutorials actually helped the sales team is an open question. However, Gummed Tapes (Pty Ltd) was a commercial success.

On one memorable day, shortly before I left the company, Sydney phoned me on my intercom and asked me to join him in his brother Errol's office, which was next to mine, along the corridor. I walked in and was asked to sit down. I supposed I was meant to observe the brothers' conversation, although it was not clear what they were talking about. In a few minutes, however, Errol and Sydney were engaged in a blazing row, which quickly deteriorated into a boxing match. I tried to separate the two rather well-built adults (who were considerably older than me, especially Sydney who must have been in his late fifties). But within what seemed like a few minutes, Sydney managed a "knockout blow". Poor Errol slumped to the floor. And Sydney, with aplomb, lifted the jug of water off Errol's desk, poured its contents onto his brother's face and walked out. I can remember, so many years after this experience, the next morning, when Errol arrived at the office, his face patched, with elastic plaster; and when asked by members of the staff what had happened to him, he replied that he cut himself while shaving. About a year later I handed in my notice of resignation and embarked on my life-long career, as a trade union official, political activist, labour relations specialist, mediator, conciliator and arbitrator. I learned much from Gummed Tapes about factory organisation, machinery, relationships especially between workers and managers and with customers, health and safety practices and useful knowledge of administration. The future for me was to be very different but work experiences are never lost.

Politics, activism and the Communist Party

I became a member of the Communist Party of South Africa (CPSA) some three years prior to its dissolution in 1950 in anticipation of the liquidation measures of the Suppression of Communism Act (passed in July 1950). By this time, the Party was well established as a legal organisation; it was the first of its kind on the African continent when it was founded in 1921. Members worked relentlessly to win support and broke lasting and significant ground during the 30 years of its legal existence. One of its most significant and lasting contributions was that it paved the way to a future nonracial democracy. Its call for a multi-racial and socialist society reverberated profoundly in the African, coloured and Indian political streams in the country. A small but devoted number of men and women of all racial classifications built a network which would play a part in creating a unique combination of vastly diverse people, who would be, in time to come, a homogenous society. It was uniquely meaningful in its ingrained belief in multi-racialism as an alternative and solution to racial segregation. After the Party's unbanning in 1990, the defeat of segregation has become a reality, and at this stage is supported by a legal framework which requires affirmative action based on two criteria: merit and or potential to achieve a required standard.

In 1947 I was an energetic, active and dedicated 17-year-old member. I would best describe myself as a serious-minded and committed communist. Initially I joined the Yeoville Branch of the CPSA, which met monthly at the home of Issy and Julia Wolfson, long-standing veterans of the trade union and political movement. Later I joined the university branch of the Party and was subsequently elected its treasurer. The branch met at the offices of the Johannesburg district committee in Progress Building in Commissioner Street. The members were mainly students at the Wits University who devoted much of their time to discussing the branch's participation in planned events for marches and demonstrations at Mary Fitzgerald Square and elsewhere. A significant interest of the branch was planning strategy and tactics concerning the Students Representative Council and National Union of South African Students (NUSAS). The membership of the branch included many impressive and strongly committed men and women, a number of whom went on to play a key role in their academic and political careers in the liberation movement. I recall some of the names, many who are now legendary: Joe Slovo and Ruth First, Lionel Forman, Harold Wolpe, Mannie Brown, Barney Feller, my brother Norman Levy, Sadie Kriel, Eric Laufer, Zena Stein, Mervyn Susser, Boetie Gordon and Percy Denton.

Like all branches of the Party, members were obliged to sell the party newspaper (the *Guardian*). Our branch members sold the paper to students but also covered Alexandra township and bus stations, taxi ranks at Joubert Park and Sauer Street. I often sold the *Guardian* in the vicinity of the Bantu Men's Social Centre in Eloff Street, Johannesburg, where there was an encouraging take up of the weekly paper. This was one of the few places in which non-segregated meetings, concerts and theatre were permitted, but mixed groups of performers were not. Danie du Plessis was the district secretary, but I do not recall much about him, except his presence at the final meeting of the legal Party. This was a really sad and historic meeting. It took place in Polly Street Johannesburg, in the large room of the Party's night school. Moses Kotane, the general secretary, and Danie du Plessis announced the dissolution of the Party on the eve of the promulgation of the suppression of Communism Act. I remember Rusty Bernstein's presence; he was angry and disdainful about the decision to dissolve the party. His close comrades, Michael Harmel and Joe Slovo, were equally annoyed and expressed their disapproval.

And indeed, it was Rusty, who a few years later, in 1953, asked to see me. We agreed to meet outside the premises of Gummed Tapes, where I was still working. It was situated near some old gold mining dumps. I was not entirely sure what he wanted to talk to me about but guessed that it was something very secret. He parked his motor car around the corner and exactly at the agreed time – five o'clock in the evening – I arrived at the appointed spot. I got into the car, and Rusty drove to a vacant parking bay, in the vicinity of City Deep Mine. I had known him for some time and often met Hilda Watts, his wife, at his house. She and I both served on the South African Peace Council and we sometimes conducted our Council business in her sitting room.

Rusty was careful in his approach on this occasion. He talked about the movement and asked what I thought about the current situation and whether I had considered whether there was a place for a new party. I grasped the nature of his questions, realising that the course of his conversation would lead to something more specific. He asked what my thoughts were about a new party, and I replied that it would be a significant and necessary move to offer better and more disciplined direction. He agreed with what I said and went on to say that a new communist party had been created (which called itself the South African Communist Party [SACP]) and he had been asked to recruit me. I readily accepted and thanked the party for inviting me to join. He explained that the secret nature of the underground party required small units to met regularly, and he would contact me soon regarding arrangements for our next meeting. This was the start of a commitment that I supported and played a role in helping to ensure its success. It was a dangerous transition from legal and open forms of active participation to the precarious challenges of clandestine struggle. Incidentally, my group – or cell – consisted of myself, Rusty, Rica Hodgson and the vocal and flamboyant Cecil Williams. We held our meetings in Cecil's flat.

Surveillance and comradeship

In the late 1940s I attended Communist Party and ANC meetings and rallies at the Market Square in Newtown. The square was named after Mary Fitzgerald in 1936 who was known as "Pick Handle Mary". She was the first woman trade unionist – a pioneer, who organised memorable strikes, especially those of the tramway workers in the 1920s. As it was with the earlier pioneers of the trade union movement and political organisations, so it was immediately after the Second World War. Trade union and political protest followed with mounting passion to advance the cause for trade union and political rights. And this contributed to the formation of what was to become the Congress Alliance, initially involving cooperation between the ANC, the Transvaal Indian Congress and the Communist Party. It was subsequently formalised in 1955 as a powerful alliance that now included the ANC, the South African Indian

Congress, the Congress of Democrats (a home to leftist whites), the South African Coloured People's Organisation and the South African Congress of Trade Unions (SACTU). This new generation of activists embraced other eager campaigners and followed the example of the early trade unionists, who led prominent strikes and ground-breaking campaigns for human rights.

In retrospect I gained much skill, experience and encouragement during this period of mounting protest. This included living and working under constant surveillance. Detectives were ever present at our meetings and took notes incessantly of what was said, as well as the names of people who were present. Initially, this was intimidating for everybody, but we grew to accept it as a standard feature of the struggle. It stiffened our resolve to defy this form of interference. In most of the political trials, Special Branch detectives handed in their notes, which were frequently so badly written that they hindered, more than helped, the prosecution in obtaining convictions. The records of these court cases will show that we were not deterred from speaking out against the regime. Our concern at the inevitable police presence of the police receded rapidly and their presence failed to inhibit us. In fact, I think it had the opposite effect of strengthening our resolve. In earlier years, this had been the stamping ground of Bill Andrews and Archie Crawford and others from the South African Labour Party who were well-known trade unionists and activists. Now, the struggle continued. This time around, the nature and complexion of the freedom fighters had changed, from the militant white workers fighting for improvements to their working condition and levels of pay to black workers who had flooded the labour market, and were demanding social, economic and political rights – especially the abolition of the pass system, and, indeed, the overthrow of racial segregation and apartheid.

Looking back now, many decades later, the perspective is more clearly defined. The tide for change was rising and larger crowds were attracted to protest meetings. They came from the overcrowded sprawling townships of Johannesburg and the East and West Rand. They were there to challenge an increasingly persistent and severe concentration of apartheid legislation, reminiscent of Hitler's Nazi discriminatory race laws which were like plagues, eating into the body and soul of ordinary decent people. Notwithstanding the outcome of the Second World War, the apartheid state was continuing its master plan to enact racial legislation, which would effectively deprive black citizens of their right to be treated as fully fledged South Africans, a practice which is now included in Article 7 of the International Criminal Court as a crime against humanity. This was both the backdrop and real situation in South Africa. It called for the commitment of likeminded people to offer support, unconditionally, to overthrowing the system of apartheid. This was my basic reasoning: a total commitment to the establishment of a state that would offer fair, equal and shared social justice. This was the rationale for our sacrifices.

And today, over and above whatever a congress member or supporter's individual ideological beliefs, this still is our fundamental desire. It is an objective which remains unchanged in our post-liberation period. This fact is, I believe, the cement which binds civil society and political parties, to make good our liberation goals and reinforce them, with solemn and binding compacts, and to lift the economy and to raise the poorest and most economically unequal of our people to internationally acceptable levels of economic wellbeing. I do not think philosophical and ideological dialogue and debate has no important place in South Africa. It very much should be present. New ideas and solutions abound – and will not disrupt our core requirement – to complete the struggle for the aims and objects of so many of the important and generally acceptable charters adopted by political groups and organisations over a hundred years of struggle for emancipation.

Many of the comrades I worked with became close friends. We met socially as well as in political and trade union meetings. I looked forward to camping with Ahmed (Kathy) Kathrada, Paul Joseph, Mosie Moolla, my brother Norman and other Transvaal Indian Congress (TIC) activists. It was the TIC comrades in particular who organised camping events and youth festivals. These were occasions that remain in my memory as special moments. India had just won its independence and we too, especially our Indian comrades, were overjoyed. The young members of the TIC were ecstatic. They taught us the songs and slogans of the struggle for Indian Independence from British rule. In 1947, Yusuf Dadoo addressed the youth festival and spoke with amazing fervour. He was regarded as our Jawaharlal Nehru. I got to know Yusuf quite well and later served on some committees with him. In the 1950s he was the underground leader (chairperson) of the SACP. He was charismatic and admired for his role in 1952 as one of the leaders in the Defiance Campaign. He was among the 8000 leaders and stalwarts arrested.

There were many comrades and stimulating friends who influenced and encouraged me. They were dedicated activists and always available for the liberation movement. Some were able to avoid detention and remained in the country for as long as was possible. Others went abroad and actively participated in the world campaign against apartheid. There was, during the most difficult years, much evidence of rising support. In hindsight, I realised much more clearly that the struggle for freedom is a never-ending work in progress. I doubt whether there will come a time when we will be satisfied with the improvements we have made. Every few decades, new and interesting generational ideas and criticisms create new perspectives on the political direction of the past and equally the present. We are, as I write, among the most economically unequal countries in the world. The important priority is economic advancement. A new generation is critical of the concessions made during the process of agreeing a political settlement with the apartheid government. And they are looking for bolder and more radical solutions.

The Discussion Club

While I was working at Gummed Tapes in the early 1950s, I was already engaged in a number of different activities. A particularly important and satisfying experience was my involvement in the Discussion Club. This was, essentially, what its name suggests: a place where young people – students, graduates, and others interested in politics, music, art, history and current affairs – could meet and discuss specific topics. The idea of establishing the Discussion Club originated with two like-minded people, Bernie Arenstein and Mannie Brown. They were well known to me as members of the University Branch of the Communist Party. We discussed the scope and objectives of the Club and invited some friends to form a committee. Bernie chaired the committee; I was elected secretary and Hymie Schles treasurer; Reuben Ruff and Ronnie Press were the other members. The Club grew and became popular. People were pleased to belong to a progressive and undemanding organisation where they could make new friends and broaden their views. It was not a subterfuge for some other body, such as a leftist party or secret society. Members accepted that, and I believe that even those who were themselves politically active rather enjoyed hearing the views of committed activists in political organisations. Over time they felt committed to it and enjoyed the social and political camaraderie. We agreed that the Club would meet every Friday night and invite a speaker. And from then until nearly ten years later, the Club continued to attract members and hold its regular meetings. There was a thirst – an important need for young people to argue and discuss new ideas. Many were students from the University of the Witwatersrand, and others had graduated and were now in professions such as law, social services, accountancy, architecture and industrial chemistry. There were also young men and women who had left school and were interested in joining.

It was a mammoth task to invite a speaker each week. The committee would meet once a month to recommend names of interesting and prominent people to invite. We gave a great deal of thought to what our members were interested in and would make contact with speakers or performers and explain what the Discussion Club aimed to do. The response from the people we invited to speak or perform was tremendous. Miriam Makeba came with some musicians from her group and sang quite late into the evening. Nadine Gordimer, who had recently written her first novel, *The Lying Days*, provided another memorable evening. The novel, which she discussed, reflected on characters and situations which were familiar to students. Eddie Roux, well known for his classic work on labour history, *Time Longer than Rope*, but also at that time a prominent member of the South African Astronomical Society, a botanist and political thinker, discussed the Sputnik which Russia had launched into the stratosphere. Walter Battis, who was a multi-talented artist, well known for his interest in Ndebele beadwork, talked about his recent work and travels. Cecily Sash talked about art and her recent work. Julius Lewin talked about African law and administration. Political discussions were sparked by Leslie Massina who spoke about current problems in the trade union movement. Walter Sisulu talked about the actions of the apartheid government and how to oppose them, while an elderly gentleman whom we always called Mr Szur, an executive member of the Peace Movement, described major conflicts in the world.

And on and on, for so many years, no matter how busy I was with other activities, I regarded the Discussion Club as special. We had a long list of members, and I would prepare and cyclostyle notices and make arrangements to post them to each of the members. Sometimes I asked Hilda Bernstein and Arthur Goldreich, who were hugely imaginative and talented, to decorate the notices. While I worked at Gummed Tapes, I managed to get the person in charge of printing documents to assist me. In addition, there was of course the task of organising transport for members who did not own cars – and there were many of them. I would contact committee members and others who had transport and arrange lift schemes. The meetings took place at Molly and Bernie Arenstein's house in the northern Johannesburg suburb of Observatory. They were immensely hospitable, and the members' subscriptions provided tea and biscuits. Some members stayed behind to wash cups and most of us made many friends and widened our social circles. Inevitably members and speakers who were prominent in politics attracted the attention of the Special Branch of the police, who followed them to Bernie and Molly's house, and noted the details displayed on the number plates of members' cars parked outside the house. The intention was to intimidate but members did not stop coming. Some did indeed struggle with the Special Branch when they sought passports to travel abroad and were asked questions regarding what they were doing at the Discussion Club.

World peace in the time of the Cold War

Another activity that I took very seriously in these years was work for peace, especially in the Peace Council. By the end of the 1940s there was an ominous change from hope to fear in the international political and social environment. Earlier, I described how closely I followed the course of the Second World War, and I subsequently maintained a keen interest in international affairs, from that time until the present. The Cold War started in 1947, when ideological tensions came to the fore, with real strains and possible conflict between the previous allies, especially the USA and the Soviet Union. The Soviet Union wanted its own atomic bomb and ultimately, with the development of nuclear technology, the hydrogen bomb. This is not to say that it would not have welcomed more socialist allies.

This indeed was a real concern for the Western powers as they were facing an increasing possibility of countries, like France and Italy, shifting to socialist positions – and perhaps – closer to the countries of Eastern Europe and Russia.

The prospect of nuclear war and the balance of power so unevenly structured was dangerous and in itself a threat to world peace. This was what we debated, as events moved on and the 1950s morphed into a furious decade of war, slaughter and dread of nuclear annihilation. And as the former colonial powers such as France and Belgium were unable to resist local pressure for liberation from colonial rule, the USA stepped into the colonial wars in Vietnam, Korea and Cambodia. Increasingly, the USA and the UK saw the challenges for independence, in Africa and elsewhere, as a threat to their own hegemony; possibly, they feared, the new independent states would turn to Eastern Europe and, more particularly, China, for assistance.

The threat of nuclear warfare, heightened by the Cold War, now became the concern of individuals and organisations throughout the world. Peace groups of prominent scholars and associations emerged and initiated campaigns for peaceful solutions to international disputes, and the levelling of the balance of power between the USA and the Soviet Union. The largest such organisation was the World Peace Council, which was formally established in 1950 in Warsaw – although there were preliminary meetings with other international organisations and individuals in 1947. The World Peace Council was encouraged and supported by the Soviet Union, which affiliated its Peace Council to it as did communist parties wherever in the world they existed. The World Peace Council was anti-imperialist and supported national independence from colonial rule. Most importantly, it advanced a philosophy of peaceful coexistence in which different political systems – socialist, communist and capitalist – could exist in harmony and negotiate treaties for nuclear disarmament.

This approach of peaceful negotiations, instead of inevitable collision, appealed to me enormously. I regarded it as an important cause and morally and essentially important to support in the best way one could. At that time of the Cold War, the notion of co-existence between two irreconcilable philosophical systems was widely dismissed as impossible. However, as time would tell, this is exactly what happened. The reality of a nuclear conflict was a frightening prospect as Hannah Arendt wrote, in 1963, about postwar technological developments which might yet make of what Hitler did "look like an evil child's fumbling toys".[9]

In South Africa Hilda Bernstein, Bram Fischer, Michael Harmel, Yusuf Dadoo, Ruth First, Harold Wolpe, Brian Bunting and many others who were members of the former Communist Party – banned under the suppression of Communism Act in 1950 – set about forming a South African Peace Council. Branches were established in Johannesburg, Durban, Cape Town and Port Elizabeth. In the months and years to come, Reverend Douglas Thompson, Helen Joseph, Salim Salie and others played a leading role. The reach and work of the peace movement in South Africa is not yet as fully explored as it should be, and I believe such research would offer an interesting take on how South Africans at that time were more consistently interested in international politics than they are today.

I retained a strong interest in world peace and did not differentiate between forms of violent political oppression, opposing it wherever it existed, in the viciousness of war situations. The absence of violence was a really significant part of my definition of freedom. In the early 1950s I succeeded Harold Wolpe as secretary of the South African Peace Council and addressed many meetings, which were mostly attended by African men and women. I worked closely with Salim Salie, Helen Joseph, Ruth First, the Reverend Douglas Thompson, Susan Stevens, Sonia Bunting, Bram Fischer, Hilda Bernstein, Babla Saloojee, Mosie Moolla, Abdulhay Jassat, Shanti Naidoo and her legendary father Narran. He was regarded as a son of Gandhi and travelled far afield within the provinces of South Africa, in search of funds to hire halls for meetings and print material on the subject of peace, and the right to oppose war without hindrance or restraint. I was a young activist of 22 years when Narran died. I attended his cremation and continued a strong relationship with his family.

We read in the World Peace Council bulletins, the British *New Statesman* and the American *Nation* and elsewhere about important events regarding peace and international stability. For example, there was the case of Mahomed Mossadegh, the elected Prime Minister of Iran who was deposed in 1953 in what we now know was the USA's attempt at regime change, a coup to preserve the rule of the shah. I mention this particularly, because the same or similar issues often arise in different forms over many generations. Within the recent past, the immediate threat of violence regarding nuclear weapons of mass destruction and allegations that the USA was seeking regime change have resurfaced.

By 1955 independent states in Africa and Asia had grown substantially and identified themselves as nonaligned to either

East or West. We were particularly interested in a conference held in April 1955 in Bandung, Indonesia, at which 29 newly independent African, Asian and Middle Eastern states adopted a declaration of Ten Principles of Peaceful Coexistence. These called for mutual respect, territorial integrity, equal rights and the settlement of disputes by peaceful means. The South African liberation movement's confidence in its own cause can be seen in its firm belief that it would in the not-too-distant future stand in line with the Bandung states. When the Freedom Charter was adopted, it encapsulated the spirit of Bandung. Among the dreams which would one day become reality, the final paragraph of the Freedom Charter states "South Africa shall be a fully independent state, which respects the rights and sovereignty of all nations; South Africa shall strive to maintain world peace and the settlement of all international disputes by negations – not war; Peace and friendship amongst all our people shall be secured by upholding the equal rights, opportunities and status of all."

I recall the Egyptian seizure of the Suez Canal in 1956 when Helen Joseph and I participated in a delegation to the Egyptian embassy in support of the Egyptian action and a peaceful solution. These were the years when empires were crumbling. I followed events eagerly as they unfolded. The French, the British and the Belgians were facing sustained opposition to their colonial rule and were conceding independence at an increasing pace. I recall reading about the French Indo-China embroilments, and the USA's role in taking them over. This was the prelude to the Vietnam War. This was at the time when the pressures of the Cold War were polarising international relations. It was an exciting period, and we were deeply involved in organising and planning the best way forward. Much of our thinking at the time found its way to the pages of publications which were established at that time: reviews from the World Peace Council and similar forums, and progressive journals and newspapers like *Fighting Talk*, *Liberation*, *Africa South*, the *Guardian* and its successors.

There was much to be read and digested about evolving aspects of Pan Africanism and more specifically the significance of self-worth. Pan Africanism was expressing itself more articulately and was taking root in different ways on the continent of Africa. This was important to explore, especially in relation to its compatibility with the principle of multiracialism, which progressive South Africans customarily embraced. What changes were needed to accommodate Pan-Africanism to nonracial democracy? We welcomed the independence of Ghana and read and thought deeply about the ideological substance of Pan Africanism as espoused by Kwame Nkrumah. (Incidentally, I was very excited to meet Nkrumah when I attended a Pan-African Congress of Trade Unions meeting in Accra in 1963 and recall his pleasant ways and diplomatic approach.) Pan Africanism was now an important aspect of the continent's struggle and in South Africa, under the leadership of Robert Sobukwe, a breakaway group from the ANC formed the Pan Africanist Congress (PAC).

Our main aim in the Peace Council was to put pressure on the government to support initiatives for peace at the United Nations and, wherever possible, consistently impress upon it that oppression leads to conflict and eventually war. Our approach was to hold meetings in halls and squares and explain that we were part of the world which was seeking peace and freedom.

There were many meetings at which I and other speakers would discuss world events. We spoke about colonialism and about countries in Africa and Asia where there were liberation movements similar to our own fighting for freedom. We also stressed the importance of world peace and co-existence to rid the world of imminent existential danger. Our speeches on these topics – or versions of them as recorded by poorly educated policemen – were produced as evidence against us when many of us were among those arraigned in the Treason Trial – subject of a later chapter.

A novel aspect of our peace work was that we organised meetings in the African townships of Orlando and Soweto. ANC members and leaders such as Leslie Massina, Elias Motsoaledi and Andrew Mlangeni invited friends and sympathisers to their homes for tea to meet speakers from the peace movement. I spent a lot of evenings at their homes, introducing them to people who had attended peace conferences in Europe or Asia. They were always inspiring and keen to impart what they had discussed at conferences and to talk about the countries they had visited. I recall driving my mini-Fiat to these townships with Ruth First, Molly Fischer, Tamara Baker, Helen Joseph and others. The peace movement in South Africa could rely on support from members of the liberation organisations. I believe that these meetings and discussions over many years added to the core values of members and supporters of the liberation movement, and that internationalism as a political aim is valid and important. If we compare that period with today's, it is clear that international problems of war and peace were discussed far more frequently and intensely by trade unions and Congress organisations than they are in post-apartheid South Africa.

While the South African nationalist government interpreted our interest in peace as a ruse to create war and revolution in South Africa, co-existence as an ideal was well on its way to becoming a world norm. Although it took many years to do so, a test ban and other treaties were agreed between the great powers. Similarly, in today's struggle against climate change, there is an important need for rich and poor nations to assist each other in seeking agreement on aid and practical infrastructural requirements for low carbon economies to combat serious changes in climate patterns. Had I been younger, I would have been a militant and active campaigner for a policy similar to co-existence, seeking solutions which would make it possible for poor and rich countries to eliminate the effect of carbon gases. At the time of writing, this is a cause for which ordinary people in most countries, especially young men and women, want governments to cooperate in finding workable solutions.

Five
My Vocation as a Trade Unionist

A new generation of trade unionists
In 1954, I moved on from my job at Gummed Tapes to the position of general secretary of the National Union of Laundering, Cleaning and Dyeing Workers (NULCDW). This was not only a shift from one kind of employment to a very different one, but it was also a crucial moment in my own life. During my years of activism – described in the previous chapter – I had developed a keen interest in and admiration for the labour movement and got to know a number of full-time organisers and worker leaders. Working as a trade unionist became an increasingly obvious next step for me, an urgent and extremely practical way of expressing my political beliefs.

But in addition to my personal desire to become a trade unionist, my move was also part of a wider phenomenon: the replacement of an older generation of trade union leaders and activists by new, younger cohorts. These were extraordinary times. The Communist Party of South Africa (CPSA) and its members – including a number of trade unionists – were among the first to bear the consequences of the Suppression of Communism Act of 1950. Section 3 of the Act required the Liquidator of banned organisations, in this case Mr J. de Villiers, to compile a list of names of those whom he considered were CPSA members. He rejected, in most instances, evidence from those who protested and disputed his intention to "name" them. Those who were statutorily named were banned and automatically restricted from participating in the political and trade union organisations in which they were employed. Moreover, they were forbidden to attend political or trade union meetings.

Many well-known and long-standing officials of the trade union movement were included, their banning orders served on them almost immediately as the ink on the gazette containing the new legislation had dried. These victims of that time are our heroes. They were men and women with strong moral values who wanted to play their part in making the world a lot fairer for all. They treasured the beliefs they held and wanted to change people's living conditions; they shared a vision of the opportunities which a democratic society could offer.

They also lived their lives to the full. They encouraged the pursuit of culture, and derived much enjoyment from literature, art and music. They used their spare time to listen to music and read about art and opera. I recall Issy Wolfson taking me to the opera in Johannesburg to hear Beniamino Gigli sing in *Madame Butterfly*. Some of the banned trade union leaders played musical instruments and lifted members' self-confidence with good-humoured song and dance. Eli Weinberg, I recall, was a good singer and a member of a Johannesburg synagogue choir. I hope perceptive biographers will revisit this scary and forbidding period to relate the life and contributions of these men and women. The achievement of their aims and legacies were our starting point. Their contributions and the manner in which they were forcibly removed resonates in the famous American trade union song: "I dreamed I saw Joe Hill last night, alive as you and me; ... I never died said he, ...I went on to organise." Likewise, history will not allow the names and legacies of our heroes of that time to die.

Persistent state action banning and removing experienced trade union leaders was now a permanent feature and would be a habitual theme until the end of apartheid. Younger generations – not only that of the 1950s, but others in the 1960s and especially 1970s – rose to the occasion, and stepped into positions for which they were not trained but regarded themselves as morally bound to help carry on from where banned, banished and exiled trade union leaders left off. It was our youth and enthusiasm which fed our commitment to the struggle. But of course, there was a price that we had to pay: fresh bannings, uninterrupted police surveillance and intimidation, and in the early 1960s detention without trial for escalating periods, culminating in the 90-day legislation of 1963. More than that, there was the prospect of no other tangible option than self-enforced exile.

This generational shift in response to state action was indeed the pattern which my involvement in trade union work followed. The well-known and much-admired trade unionist, Bettie du Toit, had recently been banned from the trade union movement (in terms of the Suppression of Communism Act) and Selma Stammelman, who replaced her as general secretary of the National Union of Laundering, Cleaning and Dyeing Workers (NULCDW), was leaving the union for family reasons. I met with Selma and the National Executive Committee and accepted the position from 1 May 1954. That was the process by which I became a trade unionist, and I would join the struggle and do what I did again if I was young and able. The cause was right and just.

In the circumstance of that time, when the political and trade union movement was under aggressive and persistent state and police pressure, it was urgent and of the essence for comrades to come forward to take the place of those who had their positions taken away from them by order of a hostile and unjust statute. Many young activists made themselves available including Becky Lan, Ronnie Press, Mary and Ben Turok, Archie Sibeko, Greenwood Ngotyana, Don Mateman, Stella Damons, Chrissie Jason and numerous others who I will say more about later in this memoir. They lived and worked in all four of the then provinces of the country and became union officials and organisers. I had met many of them, served on committees with them, and taken part in protests and activism in the political movement before joining their ranks as a unionist.

Ben Turok and Greenwood Ngotyana organised steel workers in the Western Cape; Nimrod Sejake and John Nkadimeng organised this sector in the Transvaal. In Durban, Billy Nair and his local comrades including Moses Mabhida, Kesval "Kay" Moonsammy and Steven Dlamini (a textile workers leader, who would eventually become SACTU president in exile) stepped into the fray. They organised workers in small and large towns and most importantly in sugar plantations in the rural areas of what was then the province of Natal. At one time Billy organised and managed 16 trade unions and many groups of factory workers. He was subsequently arrested and sentenced to 12 years' imprisonment in Robben Island for his membership of Umkhonto We Sizwe, the underground armed struggle. We worked quite closely in the South African Congress of Trade Unions (SACTU), before he was arrested. When I returned to South Africa, he had been elected as a member of Parliament, and was based in Cape Town, and we met from time to time. Sadly, he died in Durban in 2016. (SACTU has a key place in this memoir and will be discussed in later chapters. SACTU shaped my life.)

Throughout the country, there were trade unionists and other members of the liberation movements who were organising workers. In Transvaal, there was Gert Sibande who was affectionately known as the "Lion of the East". He organised farm workers and helped the daring *New Age* journalist, Ruth First, in her investigation (and now well-known revelations) regarding the conditions and ill-treatment of Bethal farmworkers. Hundreds of these "farm worker prisoners" were arrested on charges of infringing the pass laws which determined and controlled the free movement of African men in South Africa. Most young men and women of my generation will remember seeing police, who were attached to the "Ghost Squad", randomly apprehending black men and ordering them to stand in a straight line and show their "passes". The pass was a disreputable document that permitted black male adults to live and work in a particular urban area.

The administration of the pass laws was part and parcel of apartheid's entire administrative system. It had been *normalised* or to put it another way *industrialised*. The processes and procedures, no matter how simple or complicated, were refined to the point that it functioned as normalised oppression. White people were reared in it. Did they know what they were doing? Were they culpable of crimes against humanity? Some of us were acutely aware of it and prepared, no matter the cost, to put an end to it. Some may simply have accepted it as the norm. Others who were employed as native administration officials knew what they were doing – from the person who painted "Whites only" on park benches to those officials with portfolios to ensure the system worked. Thousands of those arrested, in Johannesburg and elsewhere, were convicted for being in an urban area without the required documentation. Many were sent to serve their sentences as labourers on the Bethal farms. Thanks to Ruth's exposure regarding their ill treatment, there was an improvement of conditions and practices.

Further afield, there was much organising activity in the factories and canning companies in the Eastern Cape. Govan Mbeki, who was charged alongside Nelson Mandela, Walter Sisulu and others in the 1963 Rivonia Trial, and spent a quarter of a century on Robben Island, made his office in Port Elizabeth available for recruitment of workers but mainly for meetings with workers who were taking part in an industrial action. Govan was well known to the political movement as an ANC leader and for his books, including *The Peasants' Revolt* on the Transkei as a Bantustan and the resistance in Pondoland. He also wrote theoretical pamphlets and managed and reported for the newspaper *New Age* in the Eastern Cape.

He encouraged us to use his office (which was in the same building as some of the unions, including the Laundry and Dry-

Cleaning Union and the Port Elizabeth branch of the Food and Canning Union. I often assisted with organising activities and helped to grow the Port Elizabeth and East London trade union branches. We worked as a team: Stella Damons, Christina Jason and among many others, the forthright and formidable, Florence Matomela was a giant of a leader who, like so many others, was militant, bold and courageous. A number of us were later included among the accused in the 1956 Treason Trial. There were many well-known organisers, such as Frances Baard of the Food and Canning Union, who addressed numerous meetings in Govan's office. Sometimes, Govan's son, Thabo Mbeki, a young student then and future president of democratic South Africa, listened to our speeches as we appealed for support and participation in trade unions and the struggle for national liberation.

Our trade union officials and organisers, as the much-recorded history of those times will show, grew to be talented and effective political and trade union activists and mentors. Soon they became inspiring leaders and their names stand linked with great landmark events, which will be discussed in other sections of this memoir. These included campaigns such as the Defiance Campaign of 1952, the great women's march to the seat of government at the Union Buildings in Pretoria on 9 August 1956, and the highly successful Congress Alliance national organising campaign for a national minimum wage of £1-a-day (equivalent to ten shillings or half a pound sterling at the time). The campaign was best known at the time by its slogan: *Asinamali, sifunimali*! – we have no money, we want money!

The activists of those times were astute and quick to recognise an opportunity to organise and increase the ranks of trade unionists. I recall their good humour and confidence and owe much to them for their encouragement and eagerness to win concessions for workers in such difficult circumstances. It was well understood that organising was often dangerous and demanded personal sacrifices; it combined dedication to growing the unions with winning tangible concessions, intervening over breaches of labour legislation, and supporting workers in their disputes concerning non-payment of statutory earnings, public holidays and overtime working. The dedication to the "struggle" of these comrades was absolute and they sprang into the fray with formidable single-mindedness in order to challenge the government's statutory removal by the banning of long-standing trade union and political leaders. The record confirms that the growing liberation and trade union movements, from the early fifties until the early sixties, lived up to and beyond expectations. Well organised and soundly supported, our actions and zeal for principled opposition to apartheid took centre stage.

This is the context of the circumstances and reasons why I, and other dedicated activists, came forward to resist the danger of the elimination of trade unionism, which certainly threatened the progressive trade unions and their allies.

Pioneers and mentors: Giants of the trade union movement

When I became an active trade union official in 1954, registered trade unions comprising white, coloured and Indian workers, were already well established. African workers had become a significant part of the labour market, although they were increasingly deprived of conventional workers' rights. The established unions had rich and significant traditions of facing up to employers: as negotiators for changes to pay and working conditions – and when necessary – taking industrial action which included strikes. They would react swiftly to unjust acts that threatened their collective agreements and solidarity with fellow unions at home and abroad. They were my role models and I tried to emulate them. I read as much as I could about their lives and achievements and met secretly with many of them to discuss practical problems in the trade unions in which they previously served as officials. I sought their advice on possible ways forward and discussed strategies regarding wage disputes or strikes. These were the banned leaders who were now unemployed or had taken up new occupations. Among others they were J.B. Marks, Bettie du Toit, Dan Tloome, Issie Wolfson, Eli Weinberg, Ray Alexander, Gus Coe and Mike Muller, all victims of the Suppression of Communism Act. They were veterans who had served the trade union and political movement. They were prepared to risk arrest for breaking their bans in order to offer much guidance and practical assistance in drafting documents and practical advice regarding campaigns. I threw myself into trade union activity with enthusiasm.

Trade union officials of their generation were meticulous in their efforts to set up organisations which would endure, even under the strains of government and employer reaction. They set out to increase trade union interest in factory organisation, health and personal safety. In some instances they established transport to and from the workplace and other practical arrangements, such as care for very young children whose mothers worked in the factories. Trade union activists and officials established a tradition of good house-keeping, accurate and timely presentation of minutes of meetings, preparation of agendas, and the convening of regular branch meetings to discuss future demands for agreements or ratify demands to be served on employers. That is how a new arrival, like me, came to appreciate and learn from past bitter battles and novel solutions. Not all strikes and work stoppages were successful and good leadership of officials and shop stewards required them to recommend settlements, which could have been won before the protest started.

These practices were inherited from early British trade unionists, such as Bill Andrews, who came to South Africa as skilled workmen. They were mentors who passed on their skills and insistence on impeccable and honest practices. They taught that a shop steward who did not always have on hand a pencil and notebook was not an appropriate shop steward. This generation of trade unionists made many sacrifices to their personal lives and well-being. They fought for better pay and conditions and much legislation for factory acts, maternity and unemployment benefits. They are on record as always prepared to confront whatever opposition to achieve urgent and much needed change. Their well-maintained records and ingrained accountability were important characteristics of sound democratic infrastructures and the prevention of corruption.

I was fortunate to get to know many of the named and banned trade unionists, whose shoes we attempted to fill. Among other dedicated, loyal and hardworking stalwarts there was Ray Alexander, popularly known as "Ma Ray". She organised workers in several industries and established successful and progressive powerful trade unions. She was the celebrated and much written about leader of the Food and Canning Workers Union and founder of several trade unions in the 1930s when secondary industries were established and expanding rapidly. Her model of an enduring and empowering trade union was far-sighted for her time. She created a social trade union, which spread its organising expertise into campaigning for housing for its members, transport to and from work, maternity leave, health and safety, and medical aid facilities. Some of these aspects of a social wage, such as maternity benefits, health and safety, transport benefits for nightshift workers, were fought for and eventually incorporated in legislation.

Soon after taking office in the laundry workers union, I also became general secretary of the Transvaal Food Canning and Allied Workers Union in 1954. By that time, Ray Alexander was already banned. I travelled regularly from Johannesburg to her home in Oranjezicht in Cape Town. I took great care to ensure that my contact with her would not give the Special Branch detectives – who were always on the watch – an opportunity to penalise her for breaching the terms of her banning order, which specifically prohibited participation in trade union activities. I met with her clandestinely, and listened avidly as she shared her experiences regarding organising techniques and what she found to be useful and effective. Her approach was novel and especially germane to the people and circumstances in the canning industry. She was an unusual trade union organiser. She literally searched for members to recruit into appropriate trade unions. She used the opportunity provided by her weekly selling of the Communist Party *Guardian* or, when that was banned, the *New Age* newspaper. She would move from house to house, and when someone appeared, she offered the newspaper and started a friendly chat. She would ask if the person was employed, and if so where, and talked about workplace issues regarding health and safety. If she observed swollen or disfigured hands or feet, she would ask about waterproof facilities, such as the provision of hand gloves and gum boots for working in wet conditions, as in the case of the food and canning industry, where workers stood for many hours each day in water on factory floors. She got to know and make friends with workers and her memory is much revered.

What turned out to be of special use to me were the times I spent with Ray in her study, late into the night, talking about her organising and negotiating techniques. She was an expert on trade union administration and the art of involving organisers and shop stewards in clear and accurate reporting back to the membership of discussions and arrangements. Ray believed that accountability was the heart and muscle of the trade union movement. She often looked to the future and talked about answerability, not only in the present but also and especially when the liberation movement would govern the country. She was wise and far-seeing. She had been well schooled by Bill Andrews, who was her mentor, and a generation later, like him, she was a mentor to my generation of young trade unionists who followed in the footsteps of the banned trade union leaders.

In addition to these invaluable accounts of her hands-on trade union expertise, she and I also discussed numerous urgent questions and complicated problems of immediate far-reaching importance. For example, there was the imminent passage of a new Industrial Conciliation Act, which had seriously detrimental provisions for black workers and extended segregation in the workplace and in trade unions. In short, the primary objective of the Industrial Conciliation Act was to separate the trade union movements along racial lines, with the aim of weakening them. The legislation (which was enacted in 1956) prohibited the registration of any new 'mixed' unions and imposed racially separate branches and all-white executive committees on existing mixed unions. The law's intent was to effectively separate coloured and Indian workers from white workers and place them in a separate trade union branch. The rights in the then prevailing Industrial Conciliation Act of 1936, which allowed coloured and Indian workers to be in the same trade union branch, were to be removed. It would close the openings or loopholes in the 1936 law, and subject African workers to the Native Labour Settlements of Disputes Act, which provided for workplace committees to be manipulated effectively into "sweetheart" unions.

These statutory workplace committees for African workers specifically excluded trade union involvement or trade union shop stewards from intervening in disputes or suggesting useful opportunities for improving conditions of black people. The legislation presented serious new problems, which we sought to challenge. The skilled jobs were exclusively for white workers. Only when the latter were not available to fill a skilled or semi-skilled job would it become available to a non-white worker. As part of an ongoing campaign against the proposed Act, Ray Alexander and Jack Simons, her husband, published a pamphlet called, "Job Reservation and the Trade Unions", which fully explained and protested against the Act. Ray wrote numerous letters and sent drafts to me for comment. The pamphlet was well received when it was published and became an important tool for activists in the trade union and liberation movement. Ray and I corresponded with each other regularly about our activities and thoughts on government actions, but, like so many other activists, dared not risk keeping our letters and notes. There was much for a fresh wave of young trade unionists to learn and gain experience. Ma Ray passed away on 12 September 2004. I recall being with her at crowded ANC election rally, shortly before she died, during which she was lionised by well-wishers.

Like Ray, Bettie du Toit was another charismatic trade unionist and also a unique person. She was a talented speaker and organiser. I began my trade union career as general secretary of the two unions which she established: the NULCDW and the Food Canning and Allied Workers in Johannesburg, the East Rand and Pretoria. The latter, which Bettie established in the 1940s was a separate trade union from Ray Alexander's, which was established in 1941 in the Cape. Bettie was known as a forthright trade union general secretary, with unique qualities. She got to the heart of a matter and would speak directly and to the point. Her banning orders prevented her from involving herself in trade union business but she always welcomed me whenever I visited her office in downtown Johannesburg, where she ran a Christmas hamper business. I took the opportunity to amalgamate the Transvaal Canning Union with that in the western Cape in 1955. Other well-known trade union victims of the Suppression of Communism Act were Gus Coe, Frank Marquard, James Phillips and Isaac Moemakoe. The latter was at one time the general secretary of the Council of Non-European Trade Unions. Other important names were J.B. Marks, Dan Tloome, Willie Kalk, Solly Sachs, Mike Muller, Issy Wolfson and his wife Julia Kruger. Sadly, Julia died shortly after she was banned. I often attended meetings at her home and frequently visited her when she was bedridden and probably in considerable pain.

I have named only a few of many trade unionists but their presence made a difference. Those trade unionists, who were deemed communists and "named" by the liquidator under the Suppression of Communism Act, were veterans who left a rich legacy of organisational and intellectual content and practice for us to carry on. We regarded them as charismatic leaders who were role models in their organisations and workplaces, shops, offices and factories. They were imaginative in making their arguments for improvements and spent much time researching for information. They sought advice from the shop floor before they submitted evidence from workers to support their demands. They fought for improvements to wage determinations which included wages, hours of work, overtime pay, late-night working and other changes suggested by the workers. They made passionate presentations at enquiries into malpractices or low standards of health and safety. When there were disputes to be resolved the now banned leaders were remembered for leading the way forward, especially on the picket lines. They used all opportunities to teach the values of trade unionism, especially the importance of solidarity on the principle of an injury to one is an injury to all. They offered leadership and hope and demonstrated the meaning of traditional class warfare, especially on the picket lines. Apart from that, they actively cooperated with wage board investigations. They were part and parcel of the work of the South African Trades and Labour Council (SAT&LC) in representing organised and unorganised workers, who did not have collective agreements and were reliant on wage board investigations to determine minimum wages and conditions of work. They were not easy to replace although we did our utmost to emulate them.

By 1954 the trade union movement was severely divided, as always, along racial lines. Nonetheless, there was a small but relatively strong group of trade unions with mixed membership, of white and black workers, which refused to embrace the ideology and practice of racial segregation. These leaders were predominately long-serving comrades, who helped found and shape the unions into role models for workers who would inevitably swell the ranks of future trade union federations. Now (some fifty or more years later), most small and large trade unions are indeed affiliated to COSATU and other trade union organisations. The named and banned leaders had served their unions for most of their working lives and supported the national struggle for equal human rights and the abolition of racial segregation. Matters of class and colour issues were equally important to them and neither of those two issues trumped the other. Both took first place.

The annals of most South African trade unions will show that they always offered solidarity and expressed disapproval of ill-treatment of victimised people wherever it occurred. They extended moral support and when it was possible, financial assistance. The progressive trade union movement continuously looked to the international sphere for innovative instances of democratic practice and opposition to injustice. It is well appreciated that South Africans are generally concerned with international affairs.

It was additionally a first-hand opportunity to be fully conversant with the culture and style of the trade union movement and its social and political weltanschauung. It was important to know and understand the trade union movement's world views, values and ideas. This was the spirit of what informed my advice to members and our consequent actions. The information was often detailed and extraordinarily useful. It provided the opportunity to jump into the "deep end" of union activity and assure members that I was reasonably familiar with past and current union issues and background to them. Moreover, information gained from studying previous cases and documents provided useful details of previous negotiations with employers and shop stewards, and included the nature and details of previous disputes and settlements and the unions participation in the SAT&LC. All this informed my understanding and helped me to use the accumulated knowledge and experience at times of significant events and the urgent need for action.

Six

My Apprenticeship: Learning on the Factory Floor

One of my comrades in the trade union movement was Lawrence Ndzanga, national secretary of the Railway Workers' Union. His wife Rita was also an intrepid trade unionist. She worked in the Railway Union with Lawrence and also organised brick and tile workers into a union. Both of them were banned in 1964. They were detained in 1969 and acquitted after a trial on charges of terrorism. And then in 1974 they were detained again, and Lawrence became yet another political prisoner to die in police custody. At a ceremony in 2017, former president Thabo Mbeki presented to Rita the prestigious Order of Luthuli for her services to the struggle. Lawrence and Rita were valued comrades and friends, and I remember that we called each other by our nicknames: his was Zozo and mine TsabaTsaba, which means "here, there and everywhere". When considering my years as a full-time unionist – as described below – I hope that readers may agree that the soubriquet was well earned.

Two laundry unions – but with one purpose

My start date at the Laundry and Dry Cleaning Union was the first working day after May Day in 1954. I decided on two priorities. Firstly, I wanted to introduce myself to our members in the factories, workplaces and depots. The second priority was to familiarise myself with what was indeed an extensive archive of minutes of executive committee and general meetings of members. These records had been kept intact from the inception of both the Laundry and Dry-Cleaning Union and the Transvaal Food Canning and Allied Workers, in which I took office shortly after entering the NULCDW. I was now working in two separate unions with vastly different cultures and traditions. The records, which were typed and pasted onto foolscap minute books, were invaluable. They were chronicles of activities, policies, political positions and past negotiations. More than that, the minutes noted in detail, information about previous strikes and disputes, settlement terms, conditions of work and campaigns to expose unhealthy working conditions and practices. A very helpful feature that I discovered in my enthusiastic reading of these past records was that they included the names of the members of the committees and individual workers in their workplaces.

A key ally of mine in the laundry workers union was Leslie Massina, at that time general secretary of the African Laundering, Cleaning and Dyeing Workers Union. In 1954 when I became a fledgling trade union official, he was 34 years old, ten years older than I was. We established a strong working relationship, and he became a valued comrade and friend. We regarded our two unions as a single identity in spite of the fact that one was registered and the African union was not. Our two unions shared a small office suite in Progress Buildings in Commissioner Street, Johannesburg. Leslie had risen from the ranks of shop steward to become not only a significant leader of a progressive trade union, but also within the liberation movement more broadly. He had been deputy volunteer-in-chief in the Transvaal during the Defiance Campaign in 1952, and in the following year was elected as treasurer of the ANC. The African Laundering Cleaning and Dyeing Workers Union was an important and leading organisation in the history of trade unions of African workers. Max Gordon, an industrial chemist-turned-trade unionist, who was a pioneer of the union movement, had revived the union in 1940. He and the Ballingers (William and Margaret) are known to have organised at least seven African unions in the 1930s and 1940s. There was so much to look back to in the organisation of African workers. They embraced multi-racial involvement in trade union activity and looked to the legal opportunities available to white workers to be included in a united trade union organisation.

Primed with what I had learned from the union's archives, on arrival at each workplace I introduced myself to the appropriate manager or senior executive and indicated that I would be visiting regularly to meet with managers, members and shop stewards. I reflect now that managers in unionised situations were beginning to become rather familiar with the sudden arrival of a new and usually young trade union official as a consequence of the banning of a previous leader. I recall being shown around laundry and dry-cleaning factories, by shop stewards and plant managers, from sections of the many and varied cleaning processes. I used the opportunities available to learn while "on the job", about the cycles of workplace operational requirements. I wanted to understand complicated problems and recognise examples of decent as well as undesirable conditions. Walking around the different workstations, keenly perceiving as much as I could, the point soon became plainly clear that organisers and officials of trade unions must understand the different job responsibilities of members. I decided that I would try to comprehend, to the best of my abilities, the multiplicity of tasks that make up members' jobs.

This was my notion of meaningful and helpful leadership insofar as workplace practices and conditions were concerned. It depended on how best one understood the minutiae of categories and the special responsibilities workers needed to do their jobs. It took some time, effort and observation to follow this aspect of specific daily operational requirements. I needed experience, knowledge and good judgment (not to mention the wisdom of Solomon) to find solutions to arguments about wages and specific working conditions; unfair dismissals; threats of redundancies; unequal application of procedures, which resulted in discriminatory sanctions concerning the same offence; complaints about job grading; and vigilance relating to deliberate management allocation of an "incorrect" grade or rate for the job. I dealt with numerous and sometimes complicated disputes, especially in respect of my responsibilities as general secretary of the laundry and fruit and vegetable trade unions. Attention to problems, complaints and members' opinions made a difference, especially to pay and living standards. Bettie du Toit pressed this point whenever I talked to her about the trade union movement. She insisted that trade unions would not grow and become powerful without good stewardship of collective agreements and following up promises. I believe that is true and that all issues are important: nothing is of exclusive concern to any of the causes we believe all are interwoven with each other.

The class struggle is always with us, and no issue trumps it. It includes the struggle for national liberation from racism and exploitation on the grounds of a person's skin colour. The one is interwoven with the other and that indeed was the difference between progressive trade unionism and the strict practice of concern only for bread-and-butter issues. Workers follow their shop stewards and trade union officials if they are seen to be challenging workplace exploitation as well as political repression. I am reminded of an example of members and supporters who demonstrated their support for us when we were arrested or detained by the police because of our political and trade union actions. I learned from experience the necessity to understand the small and large detail of workplace problems and important political actions. I always remembered Bettie du Toit's advice, which was to continuously understand workplace behaviour and to heed the importance of following up issues. Trade unionists and shop stewards spend considerable time in mediating and conciliating allegations of wrong grading and work practices. To negotiate improvements, it was essential to know and understand the significance of the manufacturing or business process in order to negotiate new arrangements or agreements. I was to learn, very quickly, that this is an important aspect of a trade union official's work. In most places of work, each job category has a specific definition. They were categorised in a hierarchical order, from the minimal task to the maximum skilled level. The established categories – and the scheduled wage for each job agreed by the trade union – became part of a collective agreement and were published by the Minister of Labour in a government gazette. Agreements were usually negotiated every year but there were occasions when a two-year or longer collective agreement was negotiated. The length of a collective contract was often the result of a deal when the parties traded concessions in return for a longer period.

In the case of the laundry and canning trade unions, we created legally binding agreements between the registered associations of laundry and dry-cleaning employers and the registered union of white, coloured and Indian workers. It was also necessary where possible to win similar guarantees for workers who were not parties to the agreement. These were mainly African workers who were not deemed employees in terms of the Industrial Conciliation Act, or workers in smaller companies, which had fewer employees than in normal enterprise. The latter were employers who chose not to become members of registered employer associations. In the event, the minister used his powers (in terms of the 1936 Industrial Conciliation Act), to extend the agreement to them. This was common practice for all agreements or undertakings in order to prevent undercutting the terms and conditions agreed. This was the loop-hole that enabled trade unions to share the same agreement with the African workers so that all workers could benefit from all the concessions and facilities negotiated.

A memorable example of black and white worker solidarity was in 1960 when the Laundry and Dry-Cleaning employers offered black workers a higher wage increase than for a large group of white workers who were categorised as depot attendants. It was a numerous category and employers were seen to be taking advantage of a situation in March 1960, when Leslie Massina and I were arrested and detained at the local Pretoria prison. We were detained under the terms of the state of emergency declared by the government, and which was triggered by the backlash of mass anger and unrest caused by the police shooting of 69 people at Sharpeville. (Details of my arrest and detention are discussed in a later chapter.) Mark Shope, the chairman of the African Laundry and Dry-Cleaning Union, took a position of solidarity with white depot attendants who were affected by this discrimination. He told the employers that black workers would refuse to accept the offer and threatened industrial action if the proposal was not extended to white workers. The employers relented and both white and black workers in the industry praised the union, and especially their fellow black workers.

The role of the Industrial Council
Over time I realised that in an unspoken way, irrespective of the attitude of employers to trade unions, officials and shop stewards are a significant cog in the wheel of the industrial process in the workplace or industry or indeed a country. The class struggle is everywhere, including in in-house negotiations and bargaining councils, and not always expressed alone in strike action. This is the case even in a society where trade unionism is discouraged or fervently opposed. It is in the nature of the industrial system and this observation became much more apparent when I was in exile and worked in the research department of the

Amalgamated Engineering Union. I represented the union at the Electronic Development Council, which was a tripartite structure involving government, employer and trade union. Indeed, a similar trade union involvement was already in place at NEDLAC (National Economic Development Council), when I returned to South Africa from exile and became aware of COSATU's greater and enhanced role in society. Government, trade unions and business were essential cogs in the wheels of the economy.

Leading the union side of the laundry and dry-cleaning industry, even in the 1950s, participation in the work of the industrial council was an important responsibility. I wanted to become thoroughly conversant with the way it worked. I needed to be innovative for continuous progress and there was much opportunity to improve our ways of working. This was an important characteristic of trade union and shop steward involvement. It is their task to lead the union side. Fortunately, for me, Bettie du Toit established the industrial council for the laundry and dry-cleaning industry in the 1940s, and it was well established as an important institution in negotiating, planning and resolving issues regarding terms and conditions of employment. Nowadays councils of this type are more appropriately called bargaining councils and they conciliate, mediate and arbitrate all aspects pertaining to an industry, especially disputes and creative settlement of problems relating to collective agreements.

I gained a good measure of skill, much practice and increasing exposure to the nooks and crannies of commercial and industrial relations happenings. An industrial council or bargaining council served its purpose as a specific mini-department of labour for the industry that it served. In this case, it served the laundry and dry-cleaning industry and other councils served other older trade unions established in the 1930s and 1940s. Most of the established trade unions, and employers' organisations used their own bargaining councils to good advantage and the inspectors became familiar with the problems that mostly concerned the trade unions. The laundry industry, as was the case with other industries, employed its own agents (inspectors) to police the industry's collective agreements and refer infringements to the monthly council meeting. These monthly meetings were important learning experiences for the executive committee members who attended these meetings but, even more certainly, for me. We had to decide on workable solutions to a wide range of problems including allegations of infringements of agreed terms and conditions. I studiously familiarised myself with the issues and supported or opposed them. It required sensitive weighing up of the issues. Mistakes can be costly and cause irritation and disaffection on the shop floor. I regarded an agreement between the trade union and employers as a solemn and binding document, which only the parties themselves may change. This proved to be an important maxim as even in post-liberation South Africa government and others consistently attempt to set aside an agreement without the agreement of the parties.

This was how the system worked. The progressive unions of white, coloured and Indian workers used their legal status to win improvements in wages and benefits for workers of all races. It was an action of multi-racial solidarity. We used the legal status of non-African workers to get the same benefits for everyone. It was a way of getting around the race laws. It was a way we could and did improve the living conditions of all workers. This process was accepted by trade unionists and the Communist Party for many years, stretching from the first Industrial Conciliation Act in 1925 until the new amendments to the legislation in the 1970s. It was regarded as the only means of consolidating legally negotiated agreements. This was a loophole in the legal system, which effectively made it possible for black trade unions to exist and grow into a powerful force. The strength and militancy of the workers helped to thwart restrictions on African involvement in trade union activity and eventually enabled them to play a major role in the trade union movement. It helped them to become a leading and integral part of the new democratic dispensation.

We were using these building bricks from 1954 to 1963 as one of the organising opportunities to mobilise the unorganised workers and protect existing unions. I was mentored well by Morris Kagan who was the secretary of the Laundry and Dry-Cleaning Industrial Council. The Council's agent, who inspected the laundry and dry-cleaning enterprises was Theo Pienaar. Morris was hugely experienced having been a prominent trade unionist in the 1930s and 1940s. Theo Pienaar was equally experienced and sympathetic to the labour movement. They tutored me well, although it was not always easy for a new and young official of a trade union to muster skill and expertise immediately. However, after a short while, followed by nine rich years of experience, I had learnt much and found my way around the block. I made mistakes, but cultivated what I regarded as persuasive negotiating skills and solid knowledge of how to successfully innovate changes to labour practices, wages and working conditions.

There were lessons for me to keep in mind, which have stayed with me for all my working life. One such lesson that I have sought to remember is that one should not readily accept "no" for an answer; instead, make sure that there is a significant reason for rejecting a proposal. One learns from experience! When I started out on my career as a trade unionist, I tended to present what I now understand is a classic reaction to a problem which occurs when one is at a loss to handle or understand an issue, and is unsure whether or not to agree to a proposed solution. In such instances, "no" was the only answer on which to fall back. I would refuse to move to a less rigid position and would instinctively answer "no". This is a matter of experience and training. Many years later, I was able to guide parties in dispute during my 20 years as a commissioner at the CCMA when arbitrating, conciliating or mediating disputes. I understood the problem and encouraged negotiating parties to "unpack" a proposal and explain its merits or otherwise. And, more than that, I learnt to use the opportunity to dig deeply to find scope to explore the issue step by step, and finally to spot the problem. This was a way of settling many difficulties at the negotiating table. There were numerous other practices derived from the experience I gained when participating or presiding over cases. I took especial care to seek explanation and the merit and clarity of suggestions.

In short, my apprenticeship in the union movement meant that I gained much experience from day-to-day activities. The days were filled with a variety of activities: negotiations, organising, attending meetings and administration. And I seldom got to sleep before midnight. I was fortunate at the age of 32 to be exposed to such responsibilities and to develop the art of negotiation and compromise without losing face, or to find ways to consensus, and even for imaginative innovation. I was becoming increasingly practised in taking a position to the limits of safety and leaving some room to avoid the consequences of defeat. Leading the union's side at the Industrial Council prepared me for many experiences at important and diverse meetings throughout my life.

Food and canning workplaces

The food, fruit and vegetable canning enterprises were different and an example of how unalike and varied personalities in different industries and workplaces are. In a manner of speaking, I cut my teeth through organising and leading the workers. The wide-ranging experiences I gathered were significant and with meaningful human and industrial experiences. This was in especially getting to know the workers individually when I visited factories and talked to shop stewards and individual members. There were a lot of union issues to talk about, but it was also good to have a friendly chat about personal things which were outside the workplace like family topics, funerals, weddings, grandparents, friends and relations who helped in the home and cared for the grandchildren during the day. There were, however, immediate and demanding workplace problems, such as a new wage agreement and innovations to improve benefits regarding, for example, transport, medical aid facilities and general complaints. And it was also fun to enjoy a good laugh about a political problem or amusing social or political happenings. At H. Jones, a major canning company based in Industria, Johannesburg, I visited the factory on Fridays around closing time, which proved a good opportunity to talk to members.

There was much that I had to teach myself in the absence of experienced union officials. Fortunately, there were comrades who I could approach for advice. But the difficulty was that many of the issues and problems were as new to them as they were to me. I had to think on my feet and, as events presented themselves in a much-changed environment, we had to become our own mentors. Other union organisers devised their own ways of handling difficult situations. Lawrence Ndzanga would wrap himself into an overall and pretend he was one of the workers in a railway depot, while he was hearing complaints about pay or working conditions. In the food and canning industry, where management was less co-operative, I devised a way of avoiding the onus being placed on the workforce for causing a work stoppage. Leading shop stewards were advised not to encourage the workers to "walk out" when management refused to discuss their complaints, but rather wait for management to react as it was commonplace for managers to precipitate a strike by ordering the workers to leave the premises. This was a ploy to shift the responsibility to the employer for causing a work stoppage. We had to create such strategies and tactics especially when there were work stoppages or protests.

Police pressure and increasing trade union militancy combined to prompt the employers – not without government pressure – to cease deducting trade union subscriptions. Their doing so had ensured that union subs would be regularly collected. So now, instead, we collected union subscriptions in the cloak rooms. Mabel Balfour, a well-known and eager trade unionist and freedom fighter, who at that time worked as an organiser in our union office, recruited members and collected union subscriptions in the female cloak rooms. And I, with the help of shop stewards, organised and recruited new members in the male cloak rooms. Friday was pay-day and there was much good humour and an opportunity for workers to ask questions or just use the opportunity to get to know us better.

The canning factories were large and there was much steam and water on the floors. So when I visited a canning factory in Johannesburg or Benoni or Pretoria, I made a special point of looking at protective clothing such as gum boots, hand gloves and head covering. They were always a vital priority for health and safety. The workstations were positioned according to operational requirements, such as the large vats for washing and boiling, and long tables for peeling fruit and vegetables. The environment was clouded with steam-mist and there was much activity. During the fruit and vegetable seasons, the factory, like the other canning factories in the country, was operated by relatively young men but mainly by women. Most were employed as temporary workers for a particular fruit or vegetable season, and some seasons required more workers than others. The industry still relies on seasonal employment of young workers, mainly women.

Each season brought new members and many became shop steward and leaders. They wanted to become involved in recruiting workers into trade unions in neighboring factories in surrounding industries. They were interested in the congress organisations in the liberation movements. In small towns, like Benoni where our branch office for the canning union was located, in the east of the Witwatersrand, the activities of trade unionists would attract neighbours and communities to assist in times of strikes and demonstrations. An outstanding source of support and encouragement person was Mary Moodley, better known to us as Aunty Mary. She lived in the Benoni township of Wattville. Almost without exception, she supported our various campaigns and protests – especially during those strikes when members of the Food and Canning Union were picketing the large factory. She lived close to the homes of many of those workers from the Langeberg fruit and vegetable canning factory. The Benoni branch of the Food and Canning Union was quite well established and Mary was militant, progressive, compassionate and practical. She sang songs on picket lines and protest marches – such as the historic march of women to Pretoria in 1956. The memory of her uplifting chant "Don't you weep don't you mourn" always boosted everyone's morale. She was born in 1913 and died in 1979. Her life story is now the subject of a university student's Master's dissertation, analysing her role and contribution in organising women into the trade union and national liberation movements. Along with Mary, shop stewards like Metha Wall and Christine Matthews, who lived in the vicinity of Aunty Mary's house, were militant executive committee members who were loyal local trade union leaders in this period of rising mass militancy.

Employers and workers were permanently engaged in disputes regarding changes in the workplace. Bosses were constantly reducing costs, often at the expense of workers' jobs. Workplaces differed according to the nature of the work situations and their diverse needs and disciplines. Over a period of time and with more experience, I realised it was important to observe and listen to the shop stewards and managers talk about their problems. It was wise only to offer advice and appropriate suggestions after listening carefully to their views. Their interactions and traditions differed according to the type of community in which they lived and worked, and produced or manufactured, or made and sold. After many discussions with workers about their jobs and aspirations for promotion to more interesting and better paid positions, they wanted a change in the way they were treated and would contribute much in ideas and ways of participating in the development of the workplace. Sometimes, there were agreements which employers interpreted differently from a trade union and a helpful amendment to work practices helped to make a difference.

Over time, I became familiar with factory organisation and how different one is from the other. A laundry and dry-cleaning factory's characteristics are usually well ordered. They have, unlike the food and canning industry, a quieter rhythm. A general observation, which I regarded as important, was that a solution to what seems to be the same problem does not always fit. Roles and relationships conform to long established collective agreements and arrangements. A steel factory requires an environment and workforce, which has a variety of skills and specifically determined job categories and work standards. Old and well-established steel factories, which have been unionised over a long period, have leaders and shop stewards who contribute substantially to maintaining smooth operating conditions.

My exposure to different work situations was an important factor in providing me with the experience to settle disputes. I had become accustomed to the individuality of workplaces and workforces. Decades later, when I served as a commissioner at the CCMA, and handled disputes which were seemingly beyond resolution, I would remind the parties that managers and shop stewards fix problems almost every part of a working day: so why, I would ask, could they not do the same at a formal conciliation hearing? This intervention invariably drew managers and shop stewards, who knew each other well, and especially the variety of tasks involving different operations, better than most, to unlock problems and find solutions or often compromises to what one believes about issues. An important observation: workers tend to let their trade union officials do most of the talking at disciplinary hearings or negotiations. But, when they are invited to comment or make suggestions about particular requirements for a job, they come into their own. They know each of the tasks, the oddities or quirkiness of manufacturing equipment and what is likely to happen in the event of operational changes, which are possibly dangerous or unsuitable.

Today's range of tribunals, arbitration vehicles and labour courts were not available to us in the 1950s when they were sorely needed, prior to the advent of democracy. But, even then, in the darkest of days, there were notable achievements by way of using the courts. We relied heavily on legal action to achieve important changes or prevent hostile and unfair labour practices. For example, we needed to develop a strategy to protect workers who embarked on strike action or became involved in protest meetings, within normal working hours. Stoppages were illegal and workers needed legal assistance. All work stoppages were unlawful for African workers. This happened often and resulted in mass arrests, heavy fines or deportations to rural areas. We found a solution when some 300 workers at the canning factory of H. Jones in Industria, Johannesburg, downed tools and after some altercation with factory managers, moved from the shop floor to hold meetings in an outside yard.

Management called the police who arrived in Black Mariah's and whisked the workers off to the local police station, and incarcerated the men and women in separate police cells. Bail was set at SA£100 per person and the trade union had to find the bail money immediately. Amazingly we did it within a few days. I contacted well-known and helpful sympathisers who were always dependable in a crisis. This was the first brush with the law that many of those young men and mostly young women experienced. They were quite shaken when they were released but kept up their spirits with songs and sandwiches. Many strengthened their friendships or got to know each other better. Overnight, new and caring leaders emerged and were looking to the union to win their case and save their jobs. On this occasion, we briefed Advocate Joe Slovo to take the case. After two days of cross examination and argument – especially the argument that the workforce did not walk out of the factory, but were chased out by management – the magistrate acquitted the accused. There was a great feeling of triumph as the young men lifted Joe Slovo onto their shoulders, singing and chanting their appreciation. All the workers returned to work and were now ready to build on their victory.

Fast forwarding to the present, I am now in my nineties and am frequently asked why I, a "privileged" white person, joined together with black people in a struggle for egalitarian, democratic and human rights. My answer is straightforward and clear. I joined because it was my struggle too. It is the reason why I stood on political and, especially, trade union platforms, and reiterated time and again, "We cannot have peace without overall democracy, equality and freedom." Indeed, this was my struggle.

Seven

A Historic Moment and New Trajectory

It was inevitable that the trade union movement, and its existing structures, would be permanently changed by the introduction of another racist shift in labour legislation, and more particularly, an amended Industrial Conciliation Act. The government was determined to achieve and perfect what it believed should be the place of trade unions in its apartheid philosophy. The South African Trades and Labour Council (SAT&LC), which was established in 1937 and included a significant number of trade unions, was split in the aftermath of controversy over the new Industrial Conciliation Bill. The bill was published in 1954 and eventually passed as the Industrial Conciliation Act of 1956. This would force the separation of white workers from their coloured and Indian counterparts into parallel branches of their registered trade unions. The 1956 legislation would also forbid the inclusion of black workers from membership of registered trade unions. The SAT&LC, which included affiliated African unions, split over many issues regarding the system of apartheid, and more particularly, the proposed amendment which among other unacceptable changes would exclude the affiliated African Unions from membership of the SAT&LC. Ambivalence or outright racial intolerance had never been far below the surface in all previous trade union federations, ever since the inception of trade unionism in South Africa.

But there remained, as there had been in the past, a progressive and revolutionary number of affiliates, who spearheaded trade union and legislative reform and were prepared to make – and indeed would make – personal sacrifices if needs be. Certainly, there is ample evidence to support this claim. We broke the conditions of our banning orders, defied restrictions which precluded our registered unions from meeting with our African counterparts at executive level, ignored our banning order restrictions on leaving the magisterial district in which we lived, organised strikes and national stay at home campaigns. We responded as best we could, to oppose and resist the provocative apartheid regime's plans to undermine and divide the trade union movement. There were no legitimate or moral lengths to which we would not go to explore and pursue our cause. We were not timorous trade unionists, who relied only on conventional trade union practice, short of turning a blind eye to accepting the status quo. We saw the class struggle in its authenticity and moved in tune with it.

The break-up of the SAT&LC – and its successors

The SAT&LC had achieved significant gains for black and white workers since its inception in 1937 until its dissolution in

1956. These were vital years, which included the run up to the Second World War and rapid industrialisation. These years saw the entry of many thousands of black workers into existing and new factories and enterprises throughout the country. Trade unions affiliated to the SAT&LC recruited many thousands of these new entrants into trade unions, such as laundry and dry cleaning, food and canning, clothing and textiles, jewellery, chemical and others. We owe much appreciation to those affiliated unions and the trade union officials, shop stewards and helpers in the SAT&LC who supported and participated in wage board hearings or campaigns for improvements such as health provisions, maternity benefits, overtime regulations, late-night working conditions, unemployment insurance and other important gains for all workers irrespective of race. But there was a predominance of trade unions and officials affiliated to the SAT&LC who were not really prepared for significant involvement with African unions. They were willing only to tolerate the membership of affiliated African trade unions in the SAT&LC but made no effort to actually help. They were not prepared to unite with them or even defend their own coloured and Indian members from segregation into separate branches. Indeed, many of the white workers in the affiliated trade unions, voted for the governing party and supported Afrikaner nationalist organisations, which were constantly banging at the doors of those unions that deviated from the apartheid notion of white supremacy.

The showdown between these groups of unions – one prepared to accept the new apartheid order of industrial relations, the other dedicated to multiracial solidarity – took place in Durban in October 1954 at a conference organised by the SAT&LC. Our group of 19 unions was opposed to the dissolution of the SAT&LC; we argued the case for united opposition to the proposed Industrial Conciliation Bill, and pleaded passionately for a united front against what was eventually going to be a continuous offensive of apartheid legislation. We were firmly determined to continue the fight for multiracialism as a non-negotiable matter of principle. Many of us took to the floor at the Durban meeting: Leslie Massina, Becky Lan, Stella Damons, Mark Shope, Don Mateman, Benny January, Chrissie Jason, Archie Sibeko and I all spoke. Archie Sibeko hit the nail on the head when he pointed out that only the organised strength of the African workers, with coloured and Indian workers supporting them, would achieve success. The thrust of our contribution to the debate was that given the vast number of unions with white and coloured workers and a growing number of organised African workers, the trade union movement as a whole would challenge the government with the advantage of its overwhelming numbers. This standpoint was undeniably realistic, but it could not succeed without united and genuine solidarity.

But we were unable to persuade the SAT&LC to fight back and defeat the Industrial Conciliation Bill which became legislation in 1956. Although on the surface there was the possibility of united action, there was no support from the vast majority of white organised workers and their trade unions. There were many thousands of coloured and Indian workers in the registered unions, but there was no way the white leadership would agree to unity of action with black workers. The majority of trade union affiliates at the Durban conference had made up their minds to accommodate the requirements of the Nationalist government and we were unable to convince them otherwise. This was an event that marked a turning point in the history of trade unionism in South Africa. After an impassioned debate, which is on record, the SAT&LC could not be saved to challenge new laws and apartheid practices. This would bedevil the country for the next 38 years. The trade union movement underwent a profound split. In 1955, the right-leaning trade unions established the Trade Union Council of South Africa (TUCSA) and the progressive left-wing trade unions formed the South African Congress of Trade Unions (SACTU).

The emergence of SACTU and its significance

There was no time to lose for our group of trade unions, which had opposed and failed to prevent the dissolution of the SAT&LC. On our return from the fateful Durban conference, the leaders of 14 trade unions formed a Trade Union Coordinating Committee (TUCC), which was committed to holding a conference to create a new trade union organisation "based upon the principle of non-discrimination on the grounds of race, colour or creed". I served on the TUCC and other members included Piet Beyleveld, Leslie Massina, J. Ohlson, John Nkadimeng, Don Mateman and Cleopas Sibande. The TUCC's urgent and only task was to prepare for a national conference comprising the 19 trade unions that opposed the dissolution of the SAT&LC. The committee was established on clearly stated terms:

> Only a strong trade union movement can fulfil its task of defending and advancing the workers' interests. Only a united

trade union movement can be strong. The interests of the African workers are in the long run no different from the interests of the Coloured, European and Indian workers... We are determined to carry on a struggle against the policy of racial discrimination and to work for the achievement of a single Trade Union organisation embracing all sections of the working class.[10]

In addition to our initial group of progressive trade unions, we were joined by unions affiliated to the Council of Non-European Trade Unions (CNETU). It was agreed that the planned conference would be convened jointly by the TUCC and by CNETU, even though the latter was no longer as powerful as it had been during its heyday in the 1940s. Preparations for the conference were impressive; the TUCC worked efficiently, and there were no major difficulties. We concentrated on popularising the idea of a new coordinating body for trade unions. We did so by issuing pamphlets to inform workers of the issues at stake, and we arranged meetings with non-affiliated African unions. After just five months of hard work, our efforts culminated in what was the inaugural conference of the new organisation, SACTU.

The conference was held at the Trades Hall in Johannesburg on 5 and 6 March 1955. It was an appropriate place for such a significant event. The Trades Hall was one of the few venues that did not have a colour bar and hence was home to generations of activists. I was 17 years old when I first attended meetings there, and subsequently used the venue for our trade union general meetings. There were many organisations launched there, as well as events, some of which I attended, such as the memorial meeting on the death of Stalin who died on 5 March 1953 and the establishment of the Federation of Women on 17 April 1954. There were 66 delegates from 19 trade unions present at the SACTU inaugural conference. Most of the trade unions in attendance had been stalwarts of the SAT&LC, and supported inclusive and equal treatment for African, coloured and Indian workers. They were fervent supporters of trade union unity of all workers and contributed much of their skill and enthusiasm. They tried to build the SA&TLC into what could have been a formidable organisation with the potential to challenge the apartheid regime effectively. But in spite of the good work the SAT&LC had accomplished, the will was not there among the majority of white-dominated trade unions to assist the growth and development of African trade unions. More than that, they did their utmost to keep the African workers in unskilled positions and kept the better paid jobs for white workers.

So, the SACTU inaugural conference was really all about the failure of the SAT&LC to achieve the objective of multi-racial trade unionism. The delegates wanted to re-enforce those ideals, which were embodied in the SAT&LC constitution for unity and advancement, taken seriously. A number of the unions present wanted to adopt the same constitution as the SAT&LC. But this was no longer the country or the world in which the former trade union federations lived. It was a different time, and the workers' leaders present at the conference talked about a sharper and wider struggle which would embrace all the people. In this case, deliverance from social, political and economic exploitation meant the national liberation of all people of colour. From now on, the majority of the delegates were prepared to make the necessary sacrifices to achieve their goal. In the event, those trade unions which did not feel comfortable with the general desire for a wider role did not affiliate to SACTU.

The looming legislation of the amended Industrial Conciliation Act, and its consequences for registered trade unions with coloured and Indian members, were the most important items on SACTU's agenda. Furthermore, the importance of organising the unorganised workers, was regarded as a major responsibility. There were many important speeches on these issues and significant discussion. There was also much excitement and anticipation for the future. Indeed, the motivation and mood of the delegates in this impressionable period, and the fervour for change, are reflected and best described in the preamble to the SACTU constitution which was enthusiastically debated and approved.

> The future of the people of South Africa is in the hands of its workers. Only the working class, in alliance with other progressive minded sections of the community can build a happy life for all South Africans, a life free from unemployment, insecurity and poverty, free from racial hatred and oppression, a life of vast opportunities for all people.
>
> But the working class can only succeed in this great and noble endeavour if it itself is united and strong, if it is conscious of its inspiring responsibility. The workers of South Arica need a united trade union movement in which all sections of rhe working class can play their part, unhindered by prejudice or racial discrimination. Only such a truly united movement can serve effectively the true interests of the workers, both the immediate interests of the workers, both the immediate interests of higher wages and better conditions of life as well as

the ultimate objective of complete emancipation for which our forefathers have fought.

We firmly declare that the interests of all workers are alike, whether they be European or Non-European, African, Coloured, Indian, English, Afrikaans or Jewish. We resolve that this coordinating body of trade unions shall strive to unite all workers in its ranks without discrimination, and without prejudice. We believe that this body shall determinedly seek to further and protect the interests of all workers, and that its guiding motto shall be the universal slogan of working class solidarity : "An injury one is an injury to all."

The conference elected a National Executive Committee and a working committee, which would meet regularly as a Management Committee to implement its decisions. Piet Beyleveld was elected president, Leslie Massina general secretary, and I was elected national treasurer (and subsequently became national president in 1956). Another member of the national executive was John Nkadimeng: he established the Johannesburg SACTU local committee, was prominent in many activities, especially organising unorganised steel workers in the Witwatersrand. John, like many of the SACTU activists, such as Stella Damons and Chrissie Jason, Ronnie Press and other unionists, joined me as fellow accused in the Treason Trial. In 1996 John Nkadimeng was appointed South African ambassador to Cuba.

The next chapter describes the task of building and growing the new trade union federation, based on these inspiring principles. But is it worth reflecting for a moment on the significance of the moment, and the place of SACTU within

South Africa's history. SACTU could not have been brought into existence without the earlier history of progressive trade unionism in South Africa – but it also broke new ground, defining new rules of engagement in the class struggle and the fight for human rights and legitimacy. SACTU ushered in a new phase for the progressive trade union movement, and in doing so transformed it into a reliable actor in the struggle against apartheid. SACTU of course sought to protect and advance workers' interests, but it insisted that demands for better wages and working conditions were part and parcel of the wider political struggle for national liberation.

By the mid-1950s African workers and their families were experiencing grim and unpalatable restrictions, relentless police harassment like the incessant arrests for pass law "offences", which led to the banishment of thousands of men to rural areas or farm jails. New legislation deepened racial and ethnic segregation and was savagely enforced. In major cities thousands of families were forced to live in apartheid-designated areas. I remember observing armed police in Johannesburg townships like Sophiatown and Newclare, which were declared "white areas", throw furniture, clothes, pots, pans and other parts of a home on to lorries; and to complete this atrocity, before moving on, they destroyed the houses with bulldozers, leaving empty square plots of red earth. The laden lorries were bound for ethnically designated areas in the massive new South Western Native Townships of Johannesburg, now of course known as Soweto.

In these circumstances it was inevitable that bread and butter issues such as wages, working conditions and social benefits – essential features of working-class struggle – would

Leon and Norman, aged four, on holiday with their parents.

Lorna and Leon with Leon's mother, Mary, at their wedding. Taken by Eli Weinberg as part of a wedding gift album.

The iconic photograph of all the Treason Trial accused. Taken by Eli Weinberg at Leon's request.

Norman and Leon entering the Drill Hall in 1956 – photographed by the police.

Helen Joseph at her garden gate at the beginning of house arrest, Johannesburg, 1962.

Chief Albert Luthuli burning his pass in Pretoria, 26 March 1960.

Yusuf Dadoo, Leon and Joe Slovo outside South Africa House, Trafalgar Square, at a demonstration during the Rivonia Trial in 1964.

With Ray Alexander and Emma at an election rally for Thabo Mbeki at Athlone Stadium, Cape Town, in 1998.

Leon, Lorna and George Bizos at the Union Buildings for the inauguration ceremony of Thabo Mbeki as President, 16 June 1999.

Leon, Pauline Podbrey, Ben Turok and Lorna at the inauguration of the Jack Simons Library, Robben Island, circa 2000.

As a CCMA Commissioner, witnessing an important agreement being signed by trade union officials and the Cape Town City Council.

Granddaughter Daisy Paterson on the Sea Point Promenade

Grandson Jonny Paterson during a chess championship match.

Leon and Lorna celebrate their wedding anniversary in Cape Town, with Emma and Mark.

Leon addresses a Centre for Conflict Resolution Meeting (photo by Armand Hough)

Lorna and Leon – back to the front!

be joined with demands for the abolition of apartheid and all unjust laws. SACTU followed this logic. We organised the unorganised African, Indian and coloured workers into trade unions, emphasising that political, economic and social advancement was impossible without the abolition of apartheid. Alongside SACTU'S slogan, "An injury to one is an injury to all", there followed the memorable phrase, "No peace without freedom from unjust laws". I recall how clearly and coherently our message reached working people. We discussed opposition to the pass system, racial and ethnic segregation and other apartheid restrictions. This was what the African National Congress and its allies were committed to and it was both practical and natural that the trade unions affiliated to SACTU should formally participate in the Congress campaigns for the abolition of apartheid. Hence, trade unionists and their unions, which were affiliated to SACTU, became activists and freedom fighters.

The necessity for this change in direction required persuasion and explanation by national and local SACTU leaders. Although there was an historical tradition for trade unions of the left to respond to unacceptable national and political issues and events, this was mainly the subject of resolutions or delegations to wherever it was appropriate. There were former trade unionists, and other political activists, who made significant contributions and personal sacrifices, now banned and often confined to the magisterial areas in which they lived. Not all of them entirely supported a formal alliance with political organisations. They wanted to be convinced of the correctness of this shift from conventional trade unionism. Our efforts to persuade them were not always successful, and they wanted more convincing. Their reasoning was mainly ideological, in that the aims and objects of the liberation movement were for liberation from apartheid, and not necessarily always appropriate to the class struggle. Some of those who opposed the shift represented by SACTU took the view that the trade union movement should not be associated with the liberation movements because police and government intervention would put an end to the carefully built structures and hard-won concessions and improvements to pay and working conditions. Nevertheless, we proceeded with the new policy, albeit that it took many sacrifices and personal hardship to become an important ally of the Congress movement. These competing approaches resonate with post-liberation debates among some trade unions today. While COSATU is in a formal alliance with the ANC government, there are unionists who currently take the view that the working class is in conflict with capitalism and should therefore opt for greater independence rather than a tight alliance with the liberation movement, which is now the government of the country.

Our stance strengthened ties between the multiracial trade union movement and the African National Congress – a process formalised in the creation of the Congress Alliance in the run-up to the Congress of the People and the adoption of the Freedom Charter in June 1955. Five organisations joined this alliance. Four reflected the racial divisions in South Africa: the African National Congress, the South African Indian Congress, the South African Coloured People's Organisation and the Congress of Democrats (which had white members). The fifth was SACTU, the only component of the Alliance with members of all races. Incidentally, in my capacity as president of SACTU I was one of the five signatories of the

Freedom Charter. The others were Chief Albert Luthuli (ANC), Monty Naicker (SAIC), Pieter Beyleveldt (COD) and Jimmy La Guma (SACPO).

SACTU and the Congress of the People

In August 1953, Professor Z.K. Matthews proposed a "Congress of the People, representing all the people of this country irrespective of race or colour to draw up a Freedom Charter for the democratic South Africa of the future". The ANC national conference approved the suggestion at its annual conference in December of that year, and in early 1954 planning began for a national convention, an inclusive assembly of all interested political parties and organisations. The Congress of the People (COP) campaign was the first formal Congress Alliance campaign since the Defiance Campaign in 1952, which had been led by the ANC and SAIC. The political climate in 1954 reflected a rising tide of interest and support for mass action and for serious political changes. In the normal course of struggle activity, this campaign would have been an important political landmark in the history of South Africa. However, its significance increased as it frightened the apartheid regime. The government and the Special Branch of the police force were more and more aware of the turbulent political atmosphere and remained ever ready to interrupt or prevent Congress organising activity.

The COP campaign, from its beginning, was different from other events. It had two distinctly different features compared with other campaigns. The first was its geographic breadth: it reached villages, towns, cities, townships, sugar plantations, factories, farms and rural communities, and involved people from all walks of life. Secondly, the most innovative tactic of the campaign was the mass collection of grievances, demands and wishes as the basis for drafting a Freedom Charter. Congress Alliance activists campaigned for about two years across the country, armed with written material explaining what was meant by their call to the people. We asked the people present at meetings to write down their demands on paper we provided and to elect delegates to represent them at the approaching COP. Many hundreds of small handwritten pieces of paper called for land, housing, workers' rights, the abolition of pass laws and of segregation. The delegates who were to attend the COP were the chosen leaders of the communities that elected them. They were known, respected and supported by their constituents – a fact that did not escape the attention of the police who did all they could to harass them at meetings in villages, factories, industrial and farming areas. Importantly, the COP campaign leadership did not indicate what type of constitutional democracy was envisioned, but welcomed suggestions from below for an alternative society which would abolish unjust laws and seek democratic social values for all the people.

The campaign was led by a National Action Council, a Congress Alliance structure, which established joint Congress committees in all four provinces. Leaders in each province formulated their own plans, which they considered appropriate to organise for the COP. Activists worked tirelessly, travelling to farms, plantations and factories to talk about the campaign. Leslie Massina and I met with the SACTU Transvaal Local Committee[11] and with other Congress Alliance activists to plan COP activities in outlying areas. I travelled to Cape Town and Port Elizabeth on trade union business, carrying with me, for local organisers and leaders, information and organisational plans devised by the national leadership of the Congress Alliance. I met with the Western Cape COP committee, which included Dennis Goldberg, Athol Thorne, Ben Turok, Greenwood Ngotwane and Archie Sibeko. In the Eastern Cape, I met with Congress activists, and trade union leaders in Govan Mbeki's office in Port Elizabeth. The number of meetings held over the full period of the campaign ran into thousands. Many details of those meetings appear in the record of the 1956–1961 Treason Trial.

The Congress for which we had campaigned was held at Kliptown, on 25 and 26 June 1955. I believe that it was one of the most important, well-considered and truly representative events in the whole turbulent history of the 1950s. We arrived at the meeting place in Kliptown early on Saturday morning, 25 June 1955. Unknown to us, some of the banned leaders such as Ahmed Kathrada, Rusty Bernstein, Bram Fischer and Walter Sisulu, who were barred from gatherings, were observing the event from safe hiding places. Congress activists had provided hundreds of benches for seating several thousand delegates. A platform for speakers was built so that all present at the assembly could see and hear the speakers. However, the start of the meeting was delayed, as we received reports that the police were stopping vehicles, which were carrying delegates and harassing them in order to prevent or delay their arrival in Kliptown. Nevertheless, most of the taxis and buses arrived, carrying delegates of different ages from all over the country. They were dressed in formal suits and jackets and wore ties as was the practice at meetings at that time and took their seats on the benches which the activists had constructed.

Speakers from the platform spoke to each of the ten sections of a draft Charter, proposing their adoption. The draft was the product of those demands collected by scores of activists from all over the country during the many months of campaigning. Cardboard boxes crammed with written demands were sorted by a Congress Alliance committee and developed into a draft charter by Rusty Bernstein and a team of journalists and lawyers. All delegates were handed a copy of the draft Charter. The sections of the Charter were debated, in the same order as the printed draft, one at a time, over two days. Delegates walked up to the platform to make a point or speak about the issue under discussion. I was a speaker on the platform when the concluding section on peace and freedom was discussed. This was a special interest to Helen Joseph and me as we both served on the National Committee of the South African Peace Council. When we concluded our speeches, delegates voted in favour of that section – as they had the previous nine. And so the Freedom Charter and its values found their way into the soul of the country. This was a great moment but, as the delegates applauded, I could see a large formation of police mounted on horses moving to surround the meeting. At this point Major Spengler, chief of the Special Branch mounted the platform and announced that he had a warrant to enter the meeting on the basis of a suspicion of a commission of an act of treason. He ordered the delegates and officials not to leave until each of them had made their way to the conference tables. They were to provide their names and addresses and hand over documents and whatever else the police demanded of them.

The delegates remained in their seats and broke into song. The singing continued until nine o'clock in the evening. They sang freedom songs and continued to extemporise other songs, which they sang over and over again. The morale was high and discipline extraordinary. In the meanwhile, the detectives required each of the delegates to hand over his or her home address and turn out pockets for documents or anything of interest to them. It was a protracted process and tense with the possibility of violence or other forms of disruption. But amazingly that did not happen, and the delegates made their way home in the darkening sky.

We were very comfortable with the sentiments expressed in the Freedom Charter. It represented the values which were talked about in and out of meetings over many years. They may not have been expressed as precisely as the written document, but they were familiar demands or values which were the subject of discussion in the liberation movement and at small and large meetings or rallies. It is important to say that there were many different strands of political convictions and beliefs in the Congress Alliance. It was and still is a broad church. It must be acknowledged that there was strong commitment and support from the Communist Party and its members, who were active and influential in the alliance. Taking into consideration the many different ideological and political strands, which were important to its constituents, the Freedom Charter was capable of serving as a blueprint for a constitutional democracy, or indeed the basic requirements for a socialist state. The Charter served as a declaration of democratic values which today are expressed in South Africa's constitution, to the satisfaction of all the negotiating parties that drafted and agreed the internationally admired Bill of Rights and Constitution.

SACTU and the Congress Alliance

SACTU not only joined the Congress Alliance but also strengthened it. The trade union movement brought energy, accountability, political training and leadership to the Alliance. The SACTU unions were growing in strength and radical determination, which was expressed in the form of strikes, stayaways, protests and campaigns to challenge the system of apartheid. Many of the young and determined organisers and officials of unions became significant leaders in their own right, who organised workers continuously over a long period and often had to start all over again when employers victimised them for joining trade unions. They taught shop stewards how to take up complaints and keep the ranks firm. They exposed themselves to personal economic, political and social deprivation and suffered bannings and restrictions on their movements, arrests and jail sentences. Some lost their lives, others had to flee the country until the forces which they helped to create achieved democracy and freedom.

Finally, SACTU's embrace of political trade unionism was an important precursor to the role of trade unions in the South African struggle. After the wave of strikes in 1973, worker militancy re-emerged, and the formation of COSATU in 1985 created a federation, which recognised the inseparability of shopfloor struggles from the struggle against apartheid. This, in turn, resulted in the trade union movement transforming into a major ally of the ANC in the new democracy established in 1994. Much was left to a new generation of trade unionists in COSATU to perfect. But SACTU had been on the right track. Its successor's strategic direction, policies and actions were similar to those which we pursued. COSATU's efforts were often hugely successful. Its policies and organisational skills were significant, and the time was ripe for it to develop and actually put the infrastructure in place to secure revolutionary changes, which we in SACTU aimed to achieve before our time had come.

Eight
Building SACTU

The task of establishing a trade union federation of affiliated unions is daunting under any circumstances. In the case of SACTU it was an historic and far-reaching event. We were aware that future generations of trade unionists would expect us to organise the unorganised workers and pave the way for powerful nonracial trade union federations in which the white workers would take their place. We no longer expected that even enlightened self-interest would persuade white workers of that time to join with the African working class to protect the rights and welfare of all workers. Numbers of the trade unionists banned under the Suppression of Communism Act expressed their shock at the demise of the SAT&LC and demanded better from a new and more progressive federation. Arnold Selby, a prominent leader in the Textile Workers Industrial Union, publicly stated that posterity would judge those who betrayed the principle of trade union unity. Similar sentiments were expressed by others: Cape textile trade union leader Nancy Dick, Isaac Moemakoe, a senior leader of the Council of Non-European Trade Unions, Issy Wolfson of the Tailoring Union, Eli Weinberg, Ray Alexander and others. What they regarded as tragic was that the majority of their fellow leaders in the SAT&LC had opened the doors wide for the Nationalist government to proceed to divide and rule along racially segregated lines.

First steps

Much now was expected from the progressive trade unionists, especially those of us who were leaders of the Laundry and Dry-Cleaning Union, Textile Workers Union and Food and Canning Union. These were the three largest SACTU unions and would be in the forefront of the new federation. They were SACTU's main source of income (through members' subscriptions) and administrative assistance. Although they were registered trade unions, they defied the law as they had always worked closely as though they were one, with African workers and unions. They had for long ignored the racial separation requirements of the Industrial Conciliation Act.

The political and trade union movement now looked ahead to a new and stronger opposition to confront the intention to divide and weaken the trade union movement. In the event, the trade union leaders were young, inexperienced and mindful of their responsibility to establish a coordinating body, which would organise unorganised workers, offer mutual assistance to affiliated trade unions and further the interests of the class struggle. It would, as an ally of the Congress organisations, focus on the shifts of the class struggle to higher, and more relevant issues of urgency. It would go all-out to organise and revolutionise the workplace for the abolition of exploitation and the apartheid system and for the achievement of a democratic and an equal society.

I recall the first meeting of our Management Committee, responsible for implementing the decisions of the federation's National Executive Committee. None of us had previously served on any executive organ of a trade union federation or coordinating body but, surprisingly, we were not totally at a loss of what to do. Leslie Massina, who was generally regarded as wise and knowledgeable, shared the experiences of the Non-European Council of Trade Unions and we benefited from this. We discussed what we thought we needed to do and, by and large, made relevant observations and some useful decisions. I suggested we establish a newspaper, and we considered the idea, approved it and discussed what to call it. It would be an organising tool, which would report on the activities of affiliated trade unions and feature articles on political and economic issues. The central theme at all times was to encourage workers to join trade unions and offer practical help. I suggested the newspaper's name had to emphasise our major principle – and so we called it *Workers Unity*. I was asked to be its editor.

There was no shortage of hard news which SACTU local committees needed to expose: the role of trade union activists and specific workers' grievances; and urgent information about government hostility, especially bans on the movement of organisers and officials, frequent arrests and recurrent raids on union offices. Of special importance was SACTU's contact with the International Labour Organization and international trade union federations like the World Federation of Trade

Unions and International Confederation of Free Trade Unions, as well as with large industrial federations of workers, especially in mining and the steel industries. In addition to our own new newspaper *Workers Unity*, there were other union newspapers, such as *Naledi*, which was the organ of the Food and Canning Union in the Western Cape. These organising tools were supplemented by many leaflets and pamphlets, such as Ray and Jack Simons' important call to action against job reservation as well as those by Moses Kotane. Bob Hepple worked with me on the production of *Workers Unity* and we received much help from J.B. Marks, Dan Tloome, Eli Weinberg and Mike Muller.

The constitution approved at our inaugural meeting required the immediate establishment of local SACTU committees to assist affiliated unions in times of trouble or serious conflict. We agreed to establish local committees in Johannesburg, Cape Town, Port Elizabeth and Durban. These committees were to become the touchstone of vitality for the new federation and would lead our campaigns to recruit unorganised workers. They were a means to strengthen and expand our support base. In Durban, for example, Billy Nair and the local committee were organising workers' committees and reaching large numbers of individuals who had not been previously organised in trade unions. The dockworkers received a lot of attention from our Durban local committee and offered much assistance during strike actions. The same was happening in Cape Town, where Ben Turok and Greenwood Ngotyana were organising steel workers. They telephoned me when there was an urgent need to persuade the employers to engage with them. Archie Sibeko, Ray Alexander, Oscar Mpetha, Stella Damons and Chrissie Jason, among others in the ANC, were likewise very actively involved in recruiting unorganised workers into the trade union movement. An important fact to note is that newly organised workers, like the steel workers in Cape Town, were frequently dismissed from their employment and we had to start recruiting activities all over again.

At an early Management Committee meeting I suggested that May Day was almost upon us, and that the newly established local committees should introduce SACTU both to trade union members and unorganised workers. They would hold meetings and take the opportunity to talk to workers about May Day and encourage them to join us in creating a powerful organisation. The Laundry and Dry-Cleaning Workers Union and the African Garment Workers Union had won May Day as a holiday some years earlier and it had been a popular victory. We had to be innovative and learn from the experience we had gained in our individual unions. We pooled our understanding of best administrative, political and organisational practices, and agreed to employ an administrative secretary who would ensure that decisions and organisational requirements were efficiently observed. Some months later, Phyllis Altman was chosen for her writing skills, administrative expertise and familiarity with the political and organisational concerns of the South African trade union movement and its international interests. This appointment proved to be well founded and Phyllis and our trade union stalwarts held the organisation together when senior SACTU officials were frequently arrested, detained or charged with one or other offence.

The notion of revolutionising the workplace was undoubtably radical. But we were organising unorganised workers into trade unions, under the ever-watchful eyes of the police and employers. We were bold and did what we could. But it was not always tactically possible to do better, without endangering the safety of the workers and wiping out the gains which we had already achieved. As we accumulated more experience and won the support of workers, we got smarter and devised ways and means of surreptitiously entering the workplace and becoming more effective. We were helped enormously by J.B Marks' organising experiences in the mining industry and the trade union. The union was eventually crushed as a result of the efforts of the mine owners, the government and severe police and army violence in the 1940s, and he was brought to trial, with others, on a charge of sedition. He shared his experience of the tactics that he and his comrades used, to assist members in the mining industry, which he successfully organised and led in an historic strike. He helped mine workers to write letters to managers, which did not look as though they were prepared by the Union and taught them how to cope with making their complaints without raising the suspicions of managers. His methods appealed to the workers and enabled them to agree to tactics to handle day-to-day injustices and win improvements to working conditions.

The outcomes of our organisational work were often fruitful but frequently sabotaged by mass arrests by the police and the prevailing political system. As I wrote in 1965, strikes by black workers sometimes resembled "small scale civil wars" with "lorry-loads of police, armed with batons, sten-guns and tear-gas bombs' – often ending when "great pick-up vans arrive and all the strikers are arrested".[12] What is more, there was the uninterrupted harassment and victimisation of trade unions and their officials, in terms of the Suppression of Communism Act.

The Minister of Justice needed only to deem that he believed the aims and objects of communism were being furthered, in order to serve a five-year ban on an individual, preventing him or her from attending gatherings of any sort. One did not have to be a communist to be on the wrong side of the river but, despite such interference, much good work was done by trade union stalwarts throughout the country. The banning orders, which were served on me were renewed as soon as they reached their expiry date. But I continued to be actively involved albeit clandestinely.

There were several occasions when I was arrested and detained, but this was not because of being found to have contravened the terms of my banning orders. We had become quite skilled at arranging clandestine meetings and were seldom caught in the act. There was one occasion, however, when I was arrested for breaching my banning order. This was on a Sunday morning in 1961 when a meeting with unemployed workers was taking place at SACTU's head office in Pritchard Street in Johannesburg. There was a familiar knock at the door, the police entered and arrested me. I was charged and detained at Marshall Square police station and placed in a rather large prison cell (incidentally, the same one that I was placed in some months later when I was arrested under the 90-day law). In a rare lighter moment, there was an amusing aspect of this arrest for breaking the conditions of my banning order. A young man was thrust into my "whites only" cell on a charge of drunken behaviour. He seemed quite sober now and asked why I was detained. I told him I was arrested for breaking a ban on attending a political gathering. Quite remarkably, he said that I was a political prisoner and must be starved of news about what was currently happening. He talked about the Profumo sex and spy saga currently making the news in the UK. He talked about Christine Keeler and the cabinet minister who was involved.

I was not sure if he clearly understood my so-called political misdemeanour nor why he foregrounded the Profumo affair in a South African prison, but I did not say so. We talked about his arrest and what he was likely to expect from the court. The next morning he was preparing to leave for court but embarrassed about the state of his grubby shirt. Fortunately, when my mother heard of my arrest, she brought food and a couple of shirts and I offered one to him. He took it but insisted that he was to return it and asked where he could take it. I gave him the office address of my father-in law, Dink Borkum, an attorney with offices near the magistrate's court. The young man was apparently discharged by the court and soon after returned the shirt. He guessed my family was concerned about me and talked about our being locked up in the same cell and assured them that I was well and not being ill-treated.

Fortunately, my case ended quickly. My comrade and long-time friend Joe Slovo defended me in the magistrate's court. He was of course familiar with this kind of case and argued that I was not actually participating in a political gathering but arranging the chairs for a meeting which was to take place. There followed a long and elaborate argument about the arrangement of the chairs which I am sure bewildered more than the magistrate. Under cross-examination, I described in a slow and longwinded way that my purpose was only to ensure there were sufficient chairs and that they were arranged appropriately. As luck would have it, the magistrate ruled that I had not contravened the banning order and promptly dismissed the case.

SACTU and the Congress Alliance

As described in the previous chapter, SACTU from the outset insisted that its struggle for workers' rights was inseparable from the struggle for national liberation and for a democratic South Africa. While SACTU's primary task was to organise the unorganised working class, it also committed itself unreservedly to mobilising the people behind their demands as embodied in the Freedom Charter.

While our present state of organisation and inadequate financial resources was clearly an obstacle, we were now formally allied with the Congress Movement and dovetailed our activities with its joint campaigns. I represented SACTU together with Leslie Massina in the Alliance's new national coordinating committee. The ANC was represented by Walter Sisulu, the Congress of Democrats by Helen Joseph, the South African Coloured People's Organisation by Stanley Lollan and the South African Indian Congress by Yusuf Dadoo. A partnership had been established, not only for that period but for the future of the struggle and beyond. Now we were better equipped both administratively and organisationally. There were more resources available for written material and information about our aims and plans. We were increasing the strength of opposition forces striving to end apartheid. We called on all members of the Congress Alliance – students, leaders, and activists – to help recruit workers into SACTU unions; and for our part, we encouraged members of SACTU unions who were not already ANC members to join the ANC. The Alliance's campaigns helped SACTU and the Congresses reach unorganised workers and simultaneously seek their support for liberation movement's campaigns.

I recall the joint Congress campaigns as significant, encouraging and largely successful. But there were lessons to be learned about better consultation with our members, supporters and constituent organisations. Mistakes were made, and these included: calling off a strike too soon; failing to involve partner organisations appropriately in demonstrations; and proceeding without the full concurrence of all or as many as possible of the constituent partners. We needed to be more skilful and learn from our successes and mistakes. The pertinent problem was that we were planning and meeting in clandestine situations with banned people who were vulnerable to arrest for infringing their restrictions on attending gatherings. It involved cutting corners.

Nevertheless, the results of our efforts are now recognised as important historical achievements. Congress Alliance campaigns included most famously the call for a Congress of the People and the adoption of the Freedom Charter; there were also the demand for a national minimum daily wage; consumer boycotts; and relentless pressure for women's rights. There was planning and organising throughout the country for a march by women to the seat of government in Pretoria. Our aim was to take demands for women's rights and equal treatment to the top of the agenda. The inclusive role of women is now in much evidence in the new dispensation, and a debt is owed to the experience gained in the 1950s from the support and vigour of those who helped to spell out the importance of women's issues. I was present in 1954 at the convening conference of the Federation of South African Women (FEDSAW) at the Trades Hall in Johannesburg. It was a memorable occasion and many male comrades helped prepare and serve food to the delegates. I remember very clearly the passionate speeches of Lilian Ngoyi, Ray Alexander and Helen Joseph, and the involvement of the delegates in the adoption of a constitution. The growth and participative role of FEDSAW and the ANC Women's League in the struggle for a new dispensation and the leadership they offered, not only to women, but all of us, is a South African example to the world of the value of solidarity between men and women. I often remarked to Lilian Ngoyi that the women's movement provided leadership to not only women but the whole country.

The concept was to inspire the people in workplaces to become freedom fighters. Helpers were given packs of written questions for new trade union recruits to complete. This was to enable us to place them in appropriate unions or establish new ones. It was truly a coalition of people and organisations with values for all that embraced the term "struggle for human rights". For example, I recall that Moses Kotane wanted to set an example of responding to our call for "all hands on deck". We provided him with the package of written questions and leaflets. He lived in Alexandra Township in Johannesburg north and was known widely as an important long-standing political leader. Other longtime leaders and seasoned volunteers did the same wherever they were located. When I visited Chief Luthuli at his home in Groutville in 1961 he strongly supported our organising campaigns and encouraged SACTU organisers in Stanger, which was near Groutville. I came to know 'Chief' as he was affectionately called during the Treason Trial. He also supported our campaigns to organise workers into trade unions in the 1950; Billy Nair, the senior SACTU leader in Natal, and Steven Dlamini, who was a textile union leader, were close to him. Ray Alexander in the Western Cape and Govan Mbeki in the Eastern Cape used their contacts to recruit unorganised workers. They were examples of seasoned organisers who, although restricted from participation in trade union activity, used their leadership skills and experience to carry on the battle while avoiding police interference.

We were gaining ground as part of the Congress Alliance. SACTU was seen to be an important partner and workers felt comfortable when they were approached by our organisers. Our method of working and consistency took a huge stride forward in the level of leadership and actual organisational achievement in the South African struggle for human rights and equality. SACTU was warmly welcomed to the ranks of the Alliance, which at that time was as strong as it was broad in its acclaimed principled views on co-operation with people and organisations who were prepared to join hands for the primary task of national liberation, which included trade union, human rights, and racial equality.

Growth, resolve and action

In spite of financial and organisational obstacles, we were making progress in establishing SACTU as a trade union coordinating body. At workplace meetings we explained that SACTU organised workers into trade unions and fought for appropriate hours of work, pay, better conditions of employment, social and political rights. From time to time there were wage board investigations, which the Labour department established, and these were of special interest to us. They investigated wages and working conditions in industries where, in most instances, there were no existing trade unions. We explained that an investigation considered pay and conditions of work such as categories of jobs, hours of work, overtime working, holidays and levels of payment. This provided for us an opportunity to discuss demands to submit to hearings. We emphasised at meetings that organised workers were in a better position to make their voices heard, and that if enough joined and supported the union a better collective agreement could be negotiated. We made these arguments at meetings during our routine organising activities; usually early in the morning before work started or when workers clocked out. We focused on recruitment in the iron and steel enterprises, assisted in organising workers in the mills around Johannesburg, and also identified other groups of workers or unions, which were now beginning to grow. In the years to come, these small unions grew relatively larger. Later, when the movement was on the crest of a wave in the seventies and eighties, they were helped by COSATU and amalgamated with other unions.

We stood up to deliberate and vindictive security police operatives and sometimes angry employer interference. But we ignored that and carried on with trade union and political activities. This was now common practice in dealing with police interference and we were becoming rather seasoned in this form of resistance. Our confidence and calm behaviour was not lost on the police or angry factory managers. They knew now that we were not going to be frightened away and instead would carry on our organising activities. An important outcome was that it emboldened the workers. They were losing their fear of employer retaliation and their defiance added to the obvious conclusion that we would not allow ourselves to be distracted by these all-seeing and ugly eyesores. The police finally realised that the political and trade union movement was determined to carry on with its recruitment and organising work. It was now clearly apparent that the police presence would be a permanent feature, particularly at political rallies or trade union demonstrations.

The role of the security police is significant in this narrative because they were never too far away. Detectives took notes of what was being said including the names of speakers and those shop stewards or organisers they had become accustomed to seeing at meetings. The mobile detectives observed us from the windscreens of their Fiat cars, which they parked, ostentatiously, for all to see. Those detectives who were on foot sat in earshot of meetings held in open spaces, with their pencils and notebooks at the ready and we reluctantly endured the presence of these uninvited and unwanted guests. Much of what they wrote was frequently presented as evidence in cases in which organisers appeared in magistrates' courts throughout the country. During the period 1956 to 1961 written evidence was produced in the Treason Trial, the content of which can be found in the trial records. Several speeches that I made were handed in as evidence. Often these handwritten accounts by police of what had transpired were admitted by the judges as evidence to be considered. However, in most instances, the evidence was slammed by our legal counsel and subsequently discarded as unintelligible. The police notes and lists contained as many of our names as they could jot down. In actual fact they knew us by name and face and could identify us in court. Likewise, we of course knew many of their names and the level of their authority.

Our apparently indifferent attitude to the police presence at meetings stiffened workers' resolve, and they bravely ignored the hostility and could be seen to be taking keen interest in the opportunities that organised workers could achieve. There were some instances when workers were concerned about our safety and were ready to protect us. The growth of SACTU was real. There were 51 trade unions affiliated to SACTU in 1961, and membership in the affiliated unions peaked at just over 53,000. SACTU unions organised workers in the food, canning and metal industries of the Western Cape; the automobile and rubber industries of the Eastern Cape; metal and textile industries in the Transvaal, and textile, chemical and dock workers in Natal. Between 1957 and 1960, unions affiliated to SACTU organised strikes and worker actions around the country. These included the food and canning workers employed by the Langeberg Kooperasie, the largest canning concern in South Africa; stevedores and dock workers in Durban and Port Elizabeth; African nurses and hospital workers at several hospitals; textile and clothing workers in Natal and the Transvaal; and employees of various companies including Beacon Sweets, United Tobacco, Bakers Biscuits and the Lion Match Company. SACTU local committees worked with the affiliated unions, and in a number of cases called for boycotts of the employers' products. SACTU briefed lawyers who defended workers taken to court.

This meant that our newly established coordinating body or federation was becoming better known. Officials and organisers were in the field on most days and visited factories and workplaces. We routinely visited our long-standing members in their workplaces and requested them to assist in recruiting unorganised workers in nearby factories and enterprises. Later, when with our Congress partners we launched a campaign for a national minimum wage of a pound a day, we provided recruitment forms and leaflets, which explained the value of organised strength. On Friday, 26 June 1959 SACTU and its Congress allies launched the national potato boycott in response to the inhumane and working conditions of farm labourers in Bethal. Over 60,000 people attended the launch of the boycott at Currie's Fountain in Durban. There were hundreds of workplaces, which were not organised and we visited as many as we could, during workers' tea or lunch breaks. Generally, we had to meet in the open air, outside the premises or in the street at the workplace gate.

We made our activities public, so that our organisation would be known and workers able to find it. SACTU officials made press statements regularly and were often interviewed by leading newspapers and reporters. In Cape Town, Durban and Port Elizabeth, SACTU local committees and affiliated unions, especially the Food and Canning Union and Textile and Laundry Union, assisted the press with stories concerning SACTU activities and numerous workers' disputes with employers. In Johannesburg, Leslie Massina and I visited factories and addressed workers and members. We were interviewed regularly by reporters from various newspapers. Benjamin Pogrund of the *Rand Daily Mail*, Hazel Fine from the *Sunday Times*, Ruth First from *New Age* and others, called at our offices for news of our organising activities – and particularly current labour disputes. In Cape Town, Durban and Port Elizabeth, Brian Bunting, M.P. Naidoo, and Govan Mbeki reported SACTU's activities for *New Age* almost every week. Phyllis Altman, our administrative secretary, was particularly adept at providing consistent news information to the South African Press Association, Reuters and trade union organisations around the world.

During the nine years I served as president of the SACTU there were difficult problem in times of disputes. Employers frequently refused to talk to union officials; in some instances, the workers who were involved in a dispute stopped work, but no member of management would make themselves available to talk to a shop steward or union organiser. A means had to be created to make contact with an effective member of management. I was by now banned, in terms of the Suppression of Communism Act from taking part in meetings. However, as I was not a "named" communist in terms of the legislation, I could legally participate in the affairs of the organisations I represented – and so could intervene in a dispute. Nevertheless, it was risky to meet with a shop steward and employers to discuss the issue involved, as my participation in meetings was prohibited. In the event, as necessity is the mother of invention, I used and steadily perfected a technique of contacting a CEO or appropriate manager by telephone. I would explain that I was the president of the South African Congress of Trade Unions, and that I was speaking on behalf of a trade union affiliated to the union. In most instances this worked, and I settled large textile strikes in Durban and the East Rand. This was actually a two-way process; employers likewise invented their own ways of approaching a thorny problem and this facilitated finding a solution. This stood me in good stead for my career in labour relations. It gave me an insight into a company's reaction to potential or actual disruption of production or other activities. It occurred to me that there was often the same confusion and chaos on both sides of the dispute. An executive or manager was mostly under pressure – from higher management – to find a peaceful solution and indeed needed someone to talk to. If the approach was comfortable and less threatening the conversation could become more confidential and positive. A lesson I learned was that a leader's success and reputation is often measured by the way he or she handles a crisis.

Learning from international examples

SACTU was committed to the ideal of solidarity with oppressed peoples everywhere and took an active interest in international developments. The leadership tried to acquaint themselves and their organised members with the major world processes of the day: decolonisation, anti-imperialism and working-class struggles for a better life throughout the world. The pages of Workers Unity and other union newspapers devoted considerable space to international affairs. Knowledge of international trade union activities was also obtained surreptitiously. South African trade unionists who were selected as delegates to conferences in the Soviet Union, Eastern Europe and China often left South Africa secretly, to avoid being detained by the South African authorities; and on their return, slipped back into the country as quietly as they had left. They established an innovative and ongoing tradition of reporting back to as many of their comrades as possible – wherever it was safe to do so. There were many occasions when meetings were organised at factories or trade union offices when delegates graphically described what they had experienced. I frequently arranged clandestine meetings at the homes of supporters in the townships. I remember participating in one of the Canning Union's routine organising trips in 1954. We were bound for fishing villages and canneries on the coast of the Western

Cape. Albie Sachs, who had just returned from an inspiring tour and conference in China, joined us (myself, Rebecca Lan, Oscar Mpetha and Elizabeth Mafeking, three veterans of the struggle). He told the shop stewards and members about post-revolution innovations in Chinese manufacturing and workplace structures. Later, I also accompanied Ruth First, Helen Joseph and others to meetings in townships when they returned from respective overseas missions.

In the early 1950s, together with others on the South African left, I followed with excitement the rising pressure on the continent of Africa for independence from colonial rule. We celebrated the victorious outcome of the people of the Gold Coast's struggle for liberation and the creation of an independent state. It was to be known by the name of its ancient civilisation, Ghana. Kwame Nkrumah became Prime Minister and the central figure in the Pan Africanist movement. It was a landmark in the countdown to decolonisation across the continent. At that point, Nkrumah was at the centre of Pan Africanism: black awareness, black leadership, individuality and self-development. The Ghanaian trade unions established the All-African Trade Union Federation in November 1959 and SACTU accepted the invitation to join as a continental ally.

Our emphasis on the struggle for independence and decolonisation had its roots in the ideals of national liberation from colonial rule and economic exploitation and class struggle. It was informed by the Marxist analysis of capitalism and the consequent struggle for socialism in the world. We fully supported the African liberation movements on the continent, which during the 1950s and into the 1960s were seriously challenging the colonial powers for immediate independence.

They were making inroads in countries across Africa, in Senegal and Nigeria in West Africa, and nearer home in Rhodesia, Kenya, Uganda and the Belgian Congo. Indeed, it was this unstoppable fervour for independence in Africa, which the USA feared. There was pressure from the USA on Harold Macmillan, Prime Minister of the UK, to expedite a programme of decolonisation in Africa. It was a tense and scary period. The Cold War was ratcheting upwards, and the USA feared that movements for African independence from colonial rule would turn to the Soviet Union for economic and military assistance.

This was the background to Macmillan's visit to several African countries in early 1960, including to South Africa. He delivered a famous speech in Cape Town, to the all-white South African Parliament, on 3 February 1960. His words reverberated throughout the world: "A wind of change is blowing through this continent and, whether we like it or not, this growth of national consciousness is a political fact … As I see it, the great issue of the twentieth century, is whether the uncommitted peoples of Asia and Africa will swing to the East or the West. Will they be drawn into the communist camp?" The apartheid government was stunned by the veracity of the speech but the trade union and liberation movements were elated. The Congress movement in South Africa always supported the struggle for independence on the continent of Africa. We regarded it as part and parcel of our struggle against colonialism, the abuse of human rights, unjust laws and the deprivation of opportunities for all the workers and people of Africa. We expressed our solidarity, with the liberation movements in Africa, on public platforms throughout the country. I recall listening to South African Special Branch detectives, reading our speeches into the Treason Trial record – and I particularly remember the words of a speech by Advocate Duma Nokwe. He fully supported the struggle for independence on the continent, and evocatively referred to the "setting sun of the British Empire". This indeed was the context in which the progressive trade union movement in South Africa was fighting at that time.

I recall the culmination of the Cuban revolution in January 1959, when Castro's forces overthrew Batista's government. We received daily news briefs on what was happening in Cuba and the thought crossed my mind: that this is what you do when you capture the post office! I also remember reading about the French Indo-China embroilments and the USA's role in taking them over. The American intervention was the prelude to the Vietnam War. But one of the most important lessons learned from international experience was in fact drawn from American history.

An important goal for SACTU was to organise workers in three major industries: mining, steel and railways. Prompted by our collective experience, and acutely aware of our lack of resources, I came to the conclusion that to do so required more than a conventional approach. It had to be the centre-point of a large campaign, which could rely on the combined strength of the political and trade union movement and would need a menu of practical and useful ideas. My thinking about this was strongly influenced by what I had read about the campaigns of the trade union movement in the United States of America and I researched the organisational methods used by the Congress of Industrial Organisations (CIO).

The CIO was born out of a fundamental dispute in the

1930s within the American labour movement over whether and how to organise industrial workers. The CIO broke away from the American Federation of Labor (AFL) and it focused on organising unskilled workers, who had been ignored by most of the AFL unions. The well-established craft unions in the AFL feared for their hegemony and the potential challenge of powerful trade unions of unskilled workers who would undercut wages and conditions of employment for skilled craft workers. The craft unions had established relationships with government, employers and other institutions which did not want to encourage the unionisation of unskilled workers, especially in mining and steel industries. The skilled workers unions were as indifferent to unskilled workers as the SAT&LC was to the organisation of African workers into trade unions. But there were notable exceptions in the AFL leadership who were determined, like us in South Africa, to organise unskilled workers. They originally operated within the AFL but ultimately broke with it. There was an obvious similarity in the tensions and debates within our SAT&LC and their AFL. As in South Africa, there was much pressure on the AFL to prevent a breakup of the united front of organised workers. But as was the case of SACTU, a split was inevitable; and the CIO was established with the objective of achieving a large scale and imaginative reach of the organised masses of unskilled workers.

The CIO's battles and hard-won organisational successes, in the 1930s, provided an example to the trade union movement throughout the world. I read much about the difficult and violent skirmishes of American workers and looked at what we could learn from them. They created organisational structures and techniques to accomplish their task and sought support from political and trade union organisation and crucially established effective working committees to oversee their campaigns. The CIO, together with its allies, were engaged in a furious struggle with employers and police. The latter, in most instances, bitterly resisted CIO attempts to organise unskilled workers all over the country. The battles with police and employers were not always successful for the CIO – any more than they were for SACTU. There were factories where unionism had been defeated and the workers were not prepared to join again; there was religious and racial opposition. Nevertheless, the experience was an historic success for the CIO and eventually the American trade union movement reunited and became the formidable AFL-CIO. This was an example of organisational technique, which had a lot in it for us. The role of the CIO, and its consequent success, is a well-documented and inspiring historical event.

The CIO planned special organising campaigns for large industrial groups and gathered support of organisations and individuals to assist. The most successful of these was the Steel Workers Organizing Committee (SWOC), which signed a milestone collective bargaining agreement with the giant and historically anti-union U.S. Steel. Our SACTU Management Committee liked the idea of special organising committees and agreed that we should attempt to match those CIO structures and create similar structures. In the light of our situation and with the precedent of the successful CIO efforts of long-ago, SACTU established three special committees: mining, which J.B. Marks headed; steel, which I chaired; and railways, which was led by Dan Tloome and assisted by Lawrence Ndzanga. We appointed special organisers such as John Nkadimeng to assist Nimrod Sejaka in the steel industry and Simelane to assist in mining. Although we did not form an industrial committee for agricultural workers, Gert Sibande organised agricultural workers in the Transvaal while Billy Nair and his comrades worked among sugar plantation workers in Natal. We invited students who were interested in trade unionism and sympathisers in the political movement to help write leaflets and memoranda. Money for these special committees was donated by international organisations such as steel federations, mining and others. We were enthusiastic and although we did not have the resources and numbers of the CIO, we, like them, had allies – the Congress Alliance – and high expectations. In the event we certainly made waves and recruited new members, but it fell to our successors in COSATU to reach the heights which we aimed at.

Nine

On Trial for High Treason

At four o'clock in the morning of 5 December 1956, two Special Branch detectives knocked on the door of our apartment at Dormax Court in Bellevue, Johannesburg. My mother, Mary Levy, opened the door and asked which of the twins, Norman or Leon, they wanted. To her horror, they answered "both". When the detectives entered our bedroom, which Norman and I shared, we asked them to produce their warrants for search and arrest. They did so with glee! These detectives had familiar faces. They had raided my trade union offices a number of times and then escorted me home to search for "illegal" documents, banned books or whatever else they sought. This time around, the search was more thorough and they opened cupboard doors and eyed the wardrobe suspiciously. There was nothing that they could find but they were doubtful. They opened the drawers widely and then turned to the mirror on the inside door of the wardrobe. We braced ourselves for a shock. For we had hidden, behind the mirror, an illegal South

African Communist Party three-page analysis of the current political situation with a discussion on the way forward. The detective rubbed his finger on the mirror, looked at it again and again, and then looked at us. He could detect no particular interest from us in what he was doing. This apparent lack of interest on our part may have put him off the scent or perhaps he was just too lazy to dismantle the mirror; in any case he decided to give up his quest. He hesitated and gave the impression that he was thinking what to do. He beckoned to his colleague, who was arduously winnowing through the books and papers on our shelves, shaking each, in the hope that secret documents would fall out. They escorted us out of the room and took us away leaving my mother weeping in the bathroom.

Inside the Fort

We were eventually taken to the old Johannesburg Fort in Braamfontein, Johannesburg. The detectives walked us through the old solidly built gates, and there we met Johannesburg activists and leaders of the Congress movement. In the early dawn swoop, they had arrested 156 of us, across the length and breadth of the country. Soon, we were joined by groups of the accused from Cape Town, Durban and Port Elizabeth and elsewhere. Of course, the accused were separated according to their racial category – white and "non-white" cells in different quarters of the prison. White accused were locked up, with three to a cell. Not surprisingly, the Levy twins were allocated a cell to share, where we were joined by a comrade from Durban, Jan Hoogendyk. We did not know Jan but were glad to have him with us. Norman and I always shared a room until we left home so were accustomed to each other's company at close quarters. We soon learned that we were to be charged with high treason and we were allocated cells as "awaiting trial" prisoners. By the time that batches of prisoners had arrived from all over the country, a total of 156 people were imprisoned – overwhelmingly members of the various structures of the Congress Alliance. Among us were 105 Africans, 21 Indians, 23 whites and seven coloureds. Ten of the total were women.

The Fort was a noteworthy old Boer military structure, a prison built by the Transvaal Republic. In previous years, it was often our first port of call when searching for a black fellow worker, domestic helper or missing friend. They might have been arrested for contravening the numerous pass law rubrics. At most times, there were at least hundreds of innocent people who were victims of random searches for pass law offenders. These were people who were known to have left for work in the morning but did not reach their homes at night. When I was in my teens I would enquire at the Fort or telephone to find out the whereabouts of people who had "disappeared". But the Fort is now a museum, and situated next to it, is our Constitutional Court, the symbol and representative of our great efforts to achieve our wisely created democracy. Since my return from exile, I have been asked to go with relatives or biographers, who were writing about people who spent "time" in that jail. They wanted me to tell them about the corridors and cells and features, which I came to know during the period I spent there. Only recently, I visited the men and women's sections of the Fort, with Qaba who is Lilian Ngoyi's grandson. He is making a film about her life and political involvements.

But on that day in December 1956, this was the first time

I had been "inside" and occupying a cell or walking up and down the passages with a cloth or rag strapped under my shoes. This was a daily chore for an awaiting trial prisoner, who was obliged to polish the corridor in which his particular cell was situated. The superintendent's inspections took place regularly and we stood to attention, outside our cell doors, eyes fixed on the floors which we had shined. There were many features which I remember, most particularly the constant clanging of prison cell doors. They were made of iron or hefty metal and their clanging had the effect of shutting out the world with the ear-splitting inevitability of confinement. I became familiar with prison facilities, the ablution blocks and certain jail smells. Sometimes I talked, guardedly, to non-political inmates. They were mostly young and always keen to know what a new inmate was "in" for. They were somewhat mystified by the reply "high treason". They had never encountered newcomers who were charged with that felony.

There were, of course, strict rules and regulations, such as daily routine inspections of our cells. We were obliged to keep them spick and span and ensure that our grey blankets were folded to bear the resemblance to an old-fashioned wireless. There were compulsory morning and afternoon walking times – each for a half hour in the prison yard. Added to this was the practice of lining up to listen to the chief superintendent's requirements or instructions to come forward if we had grievances or requests. However, despite our complaints, there were no changes to our strictly regulated condition and rations. There was not even a concession of cheap jam as some of us joked or an addition to our ration of "Katkop", the prison's exclusive, "home-made" bread, which was included in the carefully calculated calories needed for a prison meal. It is significant that the future months and years for comrades who followed in our political footsteps were different. They endured physical pain and depression. They suffered deprivation of sleep and other forms of punishment and torture to extract information. Then in 1963 detention without trial for periods of up to 90 days was introduced – and subsequently extended to 180 days.

The white treason trialists were locked up (three persons to a cell) for most of the day but were allowed the half hour morning and afternoon walk in the prison yard. This daily exercise was afforded to us – as white awaiting trial prisoners – but conditions were not the same for our black comrades. Indeed, they were packed into awaiting trial prison cells like sardines in a canned tin. When we met fellow accused at the exercise yard they were hungry for fresh news, as prisoners usually are. The first enquiry was for new information about the treason arrests and then we wanted to hear any further news about the forthcoming preparatory hearing and examination. There were many questions. When would the trial begin? What process and procedure might it follow? What was the state of our families at home who were fearful about what may happen to us? And if those arrested were parents, were their children being cared for, and how? We exchanged opinions about prison conditions concerning our "temporary home" especially the lack of books for awaiting trial prisoners; there was, it seemed, only the bible and old, out-of-date books. I read what was available but since the bible was always obtainable (by courtesy of the numerous bible societies), I read it, as did most inmates, and got to know what I had not learned at school of the old and new testaments, such as the Sermon on the Mount and the gospels. This was to be the circumstance with several other detentions and spells of solitary confinement which I experienced before I left the country for exile in July 1963.

There were three applications to the court for bail, two of which were strongly opposed by the Crown but on a third application it was eventually granted after stern argument by our legal counsel. We were in the Fort for 16 days before we were granted bail. Not surprisingly the terms on which bail was granted were indicative of the racial discrimination we were fighting against and the political purpose of our cause: £250 per white accused, £150 for Indian accused and £50 for Africans. As treason was an offence which carried the death penalty, the marathon trial commenced with a preparatory examination from December 1956 to January 1958, heard by a magistrate, which was to determine whether the case should proceed to a higher court. This was followed by the trial proper which ran from August 1958 until the end of March 1961. The relative liberty provided by being on bail was cancelled by two longer periods of detention and solitary confinement. An account of the arrests, the behaviour of the police, the raising of bail, the reaction of our supporters and the subsequent disruption of our lives and occupations is of significant historical importance. Much has been written and recorded in the archives of the Treason Trial Defence and Aid Fund and elsewhere – but as Accused no. 4 in the Treason Trial, I can vouch for the accuracy and intricate detail written by my fellow accused Helen Joseph, in her memoir of the trial and her autobiography.[13]

Incidentally, while the court proceedings were still in the Drill Hall, an interesting and memorable photograph was taken of all 156 comrades who were arrested on 5 December 1956 on charges of high treason. It turned out to be the only one ever. I especially remember the occasion as it is an important indication of the close relationship and trust we trialists had for each other. Eli Weinberg, a banned and well-known trade unionist was now a professional photographer. I arranged with him to take a photograph of all the accused to use as an illustration in *Workers Unity*. As we established at the start of the trial, any one of us with a request or interesting point or requirement could pass a note around to the rest of the accused, while they were listening to the trial or doing work of their own or writing a pamphlet. I sent a note inviting everybody to meet the photographer during the next tea break. Perhaps I was naïve, but I never thought that any of the accused might not want to come. I took it for granted they would, and they all did. The photograph is the only one of all the accused that was ever taken and is now an iconic historical document of a trial that was pivotal to the story of South Africa's transformation to a democracy. Eli assembled the accused in 12 rows of 13, seated next to the same people as in court, photographing one row at a time. He then combined the images in the correct order to create the montage that has been reproduced so many times since.

Preparatory examination

On 19 January 1956, all the accused were packed into several large police vehicles and driven to the old Drill Hall, a large, unadorned building that was especially converted into a court for the purpose of the trial. It was surrounded by our supporters from the Congress Alliance and others who joined the demonstrators. Support from branches of the ANC in Johannesburg and the East and West Rand was huge. There was a great roar with song and cheers of support from demonstrators. This certainly lifted our spirits as we saw lots of placards and banners. The air was full of anticipation. There were many journalists, photographers and newspaper reporters from several parts of the world. This was a trial which concerned governments, politicians and distinguished international legal and political personalities. Their presence made it apparent that the South African government was now under the world's spotlight and the consequences would be much greater than the regime anticipated. It stimulated the already growing international protests against the doctrines of the Nationalist government's race laws. They were now what most of the world regarded as distasteful as Hitler's Nazi Germany. The world movement against apartheid would demand a fair trial and treatment of the Treason Trial accused. The apartheid regime would have to provide substance to its charges of high treason or be seen by the world to be what decent people would so judge – a reckless and ruthless police state.

It was a serious but high moment for Norman and me: dressed in smart brown suits, white shirts and appropriate neck-ties, we walked our way into the Johannesburg Drill Hall. Standing at the entrance were two Special Branch detectives, wearing 1950s contemporary style hats and suits. They were looking at us inquisitively – something which identical twins usually came to expect. Of course, these police officers were observing the accused for their own reasons, to see that we were all present and who was entering the court. It seemed the Special Branch officers knew who we were and looked at us indicating their approval: that we deserved to be there. Unknown to us, we were photographed for police files and only after our return from exile in the 1990s we obtained a copy of the photograph, which is included in the pages of this memoir. I remember this moment vividly. I especially carried a newspaper in my right hand to hold and looked straight ahead, ignoring the presence of the detectives. There is, of course, much to explore regarding one's reactions to moments of crisis and awkward emotional situations. There were many which tested one's emotional reserves, people skills and qualities of leadership. In a manner of speaking, we learned to cope with sensitive instances while on "the job", such as in the case of the way we dealt with the police search for incriminating evidence on the morning of arrest.

Other emotional moments were how to manage prison visits by our parents and siblings – our nearest and dearest. They were close to despair and in some cases angry as they had warned of the likelihood of arrest and punishment. They feared for possible harsh treatment by the authorities and long prison sentences – and in our case, the death penalty. Each of us had his or her way of responding to family reactions in times of personal danger or difficulties. I recall the first visits of families to the treason trialists. Ronnie Press's mother and father arrived at the Fort in shock. His father did not say anything but stood aside for Mrs Press to talk. I knew some of the parents or siblings. They had not previously experienced visits to prisons. Many of them looked bewildered and worried. My mother and my sister, Goldie Abrahams, brought food and asked what was going to happen next. They were to go through this ordeal for the next seven years, during the times I was detained in various prisons – in most of these cases while the Treason Trial was still in process.

Mother and Goldie were sad and upset. Goldie must have

remembered the long talk we had, soon after the National Party under Dr Malan's leadership won the general election in 1948. She had talked at that time about the possibility of my being arrested for political activities and had envisaged the cold prison cell inevitably awaiting me. Now, during the first few days of our arrest at the Fort, we tried to reassure our families. We explained to them, with all the confidence we could muster, that the charge of treason was absurd; that we would have a strong and talented legal defence team; that we would apply for bail and return home soon. Indeed, this was the tone and self-control we developed when we were facing challenges in any set of circumstances. There were tense moments of police reaction to our presence at events, which required leadership skills to strengthen the trust and resolve of people present. Our confidence mattered. It helped to calm those who needed reassurance that we were in control of ourselves. Indeed, our confidence was infectious and reciprocated as our supporter's leadership skills gained traction.

Over time, many of our relatives, friends and family developed their own skills in coping with their situations. They brought food, clothing, compassion and whatever else was helpful. Sometimes, my mother visited court to listen to evidence and argument. She was impressed with the eloquence and substantial content of our counsels' argument. Isie Maisels was direct and hard hitting. He and Vernon Berrange continuously shattered evidence, which the prosecution presented of meetings at which detectives had eavesdropped. And, as the trial record shows, Bram Fischer and Sydney Kentridge brought their exceptional skills to counter state evidence and argument. Our legal counsel encouraged us to listen and observe carefully and we did our best to report whatever we thought required consideration or rebuttal. It is indeed important to record that over a long time many progressive lawyers, including our senior counsel, perfected their knowledge and style to defend political activists tirelessly.

The preparatory examination lumbered on throughout 1957. When it concluded in January 1958 charges were withdrawn against 65 of the accused and the remaining 91 were committed to trial in the High Court in Pretoria. The court proceedings took place in the Old Synagogue in Pretoria, and we travelled there and back every day by bus from Johannesburg. In January 1959, charges were withdrawn against another 61 accused – who were now listed as "co-conspirators" – whose own trial would take place only after that of the 30 remaining accused. Helen Joseph and I were the only white people in this group; Helen and Lilian Ngoyi were the only women. Among the 30 were comrades I had worked with closely in SACTU and in the Congress Alliance: Kathy Kathrada, Nelson Mandela, Leslie Massina, Mosie Moolla, John Nkadimeng, Duma Nokwe, Gert Sibande and Walter Sisulu. We appeared in court with a new, shorter indictment of high treason, with no alternative charges.

The Treason Trial bus was an old Public Utility Transport Company (PUTCO) vehicle, which transported us whenever the court was in session from Johannesburg to Pretoria. PUTCO buses were familiar to those of us who lived in Johannesburg and were the subject of a series of historic boycott campaigns when residents of Alexandra township walked to work and back again for weeks on end protesting against rises in transport fares. The bus arrived promptly at 7 am at a point in Sauer Street in downtown Johannesburg and arrived at the Old Synagogue in Pretoria at 9 am. At the end of each day's proceedings at 4 pm we boarded the bus and returned to Sauer Street approximately two hours later. On most days there were at least 25 of the 30 accused who used the bus as part of our daily routine for about two and a half years. Helen Joseph calculated that altogether we travelled about 22,000 miles in the trial bus. We chose our own seats. Lillian Ngoyi always sat in the front and Nelson, Kathy, Duma and I sat nearer to the back of the bus and talked. We almost always played a particular word game. We made up the rules of the game which involved calling out words and letters of the alphabet. Shortly before we reached our destination, it was usually Kathy who announced the winner, and all the passengers applauded and sang.

Sharpeville, state of emergency and a key change in policy

I first heard about the Sharpeville shootings on the afternoon of the day it happened: 21 March 1960. The trial had ended for the day and as we boarded the bus we heard sketchy news of the massacre that shocked the world. We later learned that 69 people demonstrating outside the Sharpeville police station had lost their lives, most of them shot in the back as they fled. On 30 March, the government declared a state of emergency. It affected 83 magisterial areas and under its terms 18,000 men and women of all ages were arrested, detained and held under lock and key. On 8 April, both the ANC and the Pan Africanist Congress (PAC) were banned, under the Unlawful Organisations Act which had been rushed through parliament.

The Sharpeville shootings, the state of emergency and the bannings were the harbinger of serious tactical changes in the strategic direction of the Congress Alliance. Inevitably, the efficacy of the alliance policy of peaceful resistance became a concern for us and the way forward for peaceful struggle was coming under strain. And inevitably various anti-apartheid groups were considering armed struggle against apartheid. Indeed, in the early 1960s, an offshoot of the Liberal Party founded the Armed Resistance Movement. And while there was no immediate change in the Congress Alliance policy of non-violence, subsequently, and after the end of the Treason Trial, there was indeed a major strategic change in the forms of opposition to the regime. This shift culminated in the formation of Umkhonto we Sizwe (MK), an armed offshoot of the ANC and the Communist Party. It is important to note that the Congress movement, until that time, correctly regarded nonviolence as most appropriate. It had worked well for us and inspired the Defiance of Unjust Laws Campaign in 1952; and this was followed by at least eight, energetic "all-out" campaigns using non-violent means of protest. The effectiveness of these was to be seen in additional support of new members and much improved attendance at mass meetings. The political tide was rising, and the apartheid government knew this. It countered it with police violence, arrests and addition punitive legislation such as the ill-reputed General Law Amendment Act (the 90-day law) which enabled the Special Branch of the police to "sweep up" key organisers and activists without charge or trial for 90 days at a time. The Treason Trial was a key feature of the state's response to the intensifying current of anti-apartheid opposition.

MK would eventually become relevant in the passing of political power to a democratic dispensation. It would inevitably feature in the history syllabuses of post-liberation studies; my grandchildren Jonny and Daisy would write about MK in their history classes at school. The change in policy in 1961 permitted armed struggle, the use of violence, provided that it was for hard targets such as strategic installations but not soft targets which involved the vulnerability of people. The change required to be handled carefully as it did not, for a while, sit comfortably with some leaders but they did not repudiate it. I supported the decision for a continuation of the struggle in the manner we were accustomed alongside a strategy of sabotage of strategic resources and a strict policy of avoiding harm to individuals.

Nevertheless, I did not participate in the work of MK. My role was in active, open trade union organisation. The Communist Party was a principal supporter of MK and was preparing its followers for a political change in direction. It maintained close touch with its members for the shift in policy and prepared us for illegal operations. We trained to use the roof gardens of buildings to drop leaflet "bombs" and those members of the party who joined the armed struggle led by Nelson Mandela and Oliver Tambo played a significant role. I knew many MK members who fought bravely and died in the 30-year armed struggle to end the illegitimate apartheid regime.

In detention while on trial

On 30 March, there was once again that well-known early morning knock on the door. When I opened it, there stood those unmistakably regular Special Branch detectives. They produced a warrant authorising my arrest in terms of the provisions of a state of emergency declared by the government.

My mother, who was alarmed and troubled, came to the front door to say goodbye. I cannot remember whether I kissed her or what comforting words I said but it was an awful moment. I had considered the consequences of this kind of upheaval and in some way prepared myself for it but did not share my thoughts. In retrospect I believe that our nearest and dearest did not always share their fear of the unknown or discuss the damage, both emotional and otherwise, which they suffered. Activists expected to be "picked up" but did not always discuss it openly and I regret this; although I realise that we operated clandestinely and secrecy was an essential element. It was safer for everybody to be careful about what they said. Later that year, while I was being held in the Pretoria Local Prison, I remember my mother making one of her brave and sad visits to see me. She told me that had heard the detainees were contemplating hunger strikes and wanted to know if I would be participating. What could I say? As I write this memoir at the age of almost 93 years, I confess there were tears in my eyes. (We did conduct a hunger strike in protest against the conditions in which we were being held and I did participate. Helen Joseph later recalled: "We gathered round at Court on Leon Levy's tenth day, fascinated to watch him break his fast with a Marie biscuit, a look of sheer ecstasy on his face".[14])

We were moved from Johannesburg to the Pretoria Local Prison, which is where the state of emergency detainees were held. The majority of the detainees were kept in jail for three months, but the treason trialists had to wait for their release for a further two months until the state of emergency ended. As I was the only white man out of the 30 accused in the second indictment, 1 was held in solitary confinement for the two additional months until the state of emergency was formerly ended. The other non-white males who were accused of high treason were held in another wing of the building. Chief Luthuli, who was initially in the first indictment but "dropped" pending the outcome of the second indictment, was one of our major witnesses. Irrespective of that and notwithstanding his serious condition of high blood pressure, he was detained during the state of emergency. He was held in the hospital wing of the jail adjacent to the large dormitory, which eventually became the temporary "home" of all the white male detainees rounded up at the start of the state of emergency. Helen, Lilian and other women treason trialists were detained in the women's section, which was situated in a different building.

There was a prison for black women and a separate one for white women. More than that, in the nature of the apartheid system, there were other requirements. Helen, the only white woman, was transported in a separate police van to and from the court. However, before she could be driven to special court at the Old Synagogue the only white-skinned male treason trialist – me – had to be fetched from the men's prison. Both of us were seated in the front of the van next to the driver, who was a warder from Pretoria Local. The significance of this account of these routine transport arrangements is heightened by the fact that Chief Luthuli was a special passenger who was included in this daily slog backwards and forwards to the various prisons. He was one of our star witnesses. and was responding to questions from our counsel and the prosecution. Chief's evidence is of course available in the trial record. It was learned, knowledgeable and replete with ANC history, particularly the non-violent struggle for the abolition of apartheid. He talked about the peaceful nature of each of the campaigns against the system of apartheid. As a detainee, in terms of the state of emergency, he was placed with Helen and me in the vehicle that transported us to the local prison. However, he was obliged by the conventions of apartheid to sit at the back of the prison van, quite separately from us and out of earshot.

On one morning, while I was escorted by the young white warder who usually took me to the police vehicle, I asked him to let me sit at the back with Chief Luthuli to discuss his health. This request was very irregular, but the young warder had become friendlier and was soon to go on a training course. He agreed and let me sit at the back of the van. As it drove off, I explained to Chief that I had asked to sit at the back to enquire about his health but that was not the only reason. I told him that I had some excellent confidential news for him. He perked up, smiled and asked what it was. I told him that I was tasked to share a confidence with him. (It was Advocate Bram Fischer who entrusted this message to me.) Chief Luthuli was to be awarded the Nobel Peace Prize for his contribution to the cause of human rights and leadership in seeking the abolition of racist laws and discrimination by non-violent peaceful struggle. His immediate reaction was: "We all won it – the prize is for all of us." I understood what he was saying but stressed it really was for him and well deserved. I shook his hand and when we reached the Old Synagogue, he presented himself for examination as a witness and I joined Helen and walked to our well-worn seats to listen to the day's proceedings.

The period of detention in this state of emergency was hectic for the treason trialists: in addition to the privations of detention we now took on a new active role in the court hearings. Our legal counsel was concerned that witnesses might fear reprisals or arrest resulting from their testimony. An additional concern was that the conduct and manner of the trial would be prejudiced while the state of emergency persisted. On behalf of the 30 of us, Accused No. 6 – Advocate Duma Nokwe – addressed the court with the support of our legal counsel. He stated that formal notice had been given that we would defend ourselves until the end of the state of emergency and dispense with our legal team. Much has already been written about the expertise and professional contribution of the leader of our legal counsel, Isie Maisels and the invaluable legal contribution of his team. Now, he addressed the court: "We have no further mandate and we will consequently not trouble Your Lordships any further" – and he and his team left the courtroom. They returned at the end of the state of emergency, but for the rest of its duration it was different members of the accused who were called as witnesses, and others who cross-examined them.

I attended court when it was in session but there were many adjournments and we spent much time in detention preparing our defence. The "non-white" cells were not far away from the quarters of the white detainees. Indeed, the trial was now of world-wide concern and the government needed to ensure it was seen to be fair. Consequently, in the daytime or the evening, after court hearings if the court was in session, I was allowed to leave the large dormitory, which was now my "temporary home" to meet with black male trialists to prepare our defence. This must have been a very rare occasion in South African history when white accused were allowed to meet with black fellow co-accused in the same prison cells. This continued for the duration of the state of emergency until the return of our legal counsel later on 26 August 1960. We gained many legal and political lessons including the ability of carefully examining our witnesses on details of activities but clearly avoiding issues of policy. Policy issues were especially reserved for the expertise of our defence counsel when they resumed their role.

I was escorted each time by a prison warder to my fellow accused who were detained in the "non-white" section of the local prison. Their cells were packed with detainees who were arrested under the state of emergency. Most of them were young and politically active. Some were members or supporters of the Pan Africanist Congress but a large number were ANC followers or members. Many of the detainees in the non-white prison cells wore prison grey blankets over their clothes to keep warm; the season was changing, and cold spells were beginning to creep in. I was taken to the prison cells where the Treason Trial accused were being prepared by Nelson Mandela and Duma Nokwe to lead some of us as witnesses or preparing to testify on the activities of the Congress Alliance and the Peace Council. Nelson and Duma, Accused Nos 6 and 16, were well known as lawyers and admired for their charismatic leadership and skill in challenging the authorities. We were fortunate to have them coach us.

We spent a considerable time discussing questions and what responses we were likely to have to reflect on. The South African Peace Council was included in the indictment as one of the organisations conspiring to overthrow the state by force and violence and establish a communist state. As I was the secretary of the Peace Council in addition to my trade union and Congress Alliance activities, it was appropriate for me to put questions to Helen Joseph. She had been for several years and still was a leading member of the Peace Council. Others of us who were members and active campaigners were Ahmed Kathrada, Mosie Moolla and Farid Adams; they participated in the discussion with Nelson and Duma on the Peace Council and the campaigns and speeches that Special Branch detectives had already put on the court record in the early days of the trial. We agreed on a line of questions I would put to Helen Joseph. The next day in court I cross-examined her for a full day, carefully putting to her the questions which we had discussed, which included my role in the Peace Council and our activities. It was a daunting experience for me, although Helen later wrote kindly of my performance: Leon posed "deliberately, carefully phrased questions with an aplomb to be envied by many an advocate, and maintaining an imperturbability which had to be seen to be believed".[15] Helen excelled herself in the witness stand and proved one of our most impressive and important witnesses.

Other comrades, who were questioned by fellow accused and members of the different Congress organisations, gave evidence or answered questions regarding Congress Alliance campaigns. They told the court about demonstrated remarkable organising skills and a complete and wide-ranging understanding of the history, nature and political scope of our cause. The trial record highlights our political and philosophical positions and clearly indicated that we knew and understood the aims and objectives of our activities. Moreover the evidence was truthful and impressive and clearly indicated our nonviolent militancy. It is noteworthy to recall that after Nelson Mandela was released from prison in 1990, Presiding Judge Rumpff presented him with finely bound copies of the voluminous trial record. I believe the spirited and rich defence led by remarkable legal giants is more than a trial record; it is a rich and truthful history of a period of time in the struggle for liberation and democracy.

The Treason Trial as classroom

I believe that the accused learnt a considerable amount from their exposure to legal issues and arguments regarding important evidence, and from tense and difficult moments in the witness stand. The trial ran from December 1956 to March 1961 – and that long period was indeed our "graduating years". The experience brought us closer to one another. We inevitably bonded into a group in which we worked, planned and socialised. We had in the course of things inevitably become more tested and strengthened. The impact of the trial on my life had the effect of increasing my self-confidence and commitment to continue despite and indeed because of the importance of radical resistance. We offered a crucial and pivotal political contribution. Our cause was for values regarding human rights – and these values were abiding. We confronted issues of civil liberties and all forms of inequality.

I stress the importance of this because there are generational questions being asked 25 years into our democratic dispensation. Committed democrats ask whether they – and we – are disillusioned by the state capture perpetrated by criminal elements within the post-apartheid government and elsewhere. I certainly am angered and disappointed by the theft, corruption and dishonesty, which have stained the name of the liberation movement and weakened trust in it. More than that, it has deprived the country of resources to expand the economy and to improve the wellbeing of millions of South Africans. However, my struggle was about freedom, and particularly concerned with the abolition of apartheid – that "crime against humanity", which destroyed so many dreams – and with people's entitlement to a life free from the abuse of human rights. If needed I would certainly offer myself again to uphold the principles and achievements of our struggle. That was my vision and what mattered was the method and political work which was required to achieve the democratic destiny of South Africa.

In the periods during the trial that I was on bail, I continued to pursue my trade union responsibilities as best I could. I would work before and after court sessions and at weekends, dealing with trade union matters, and visiting SACTU's headquarters in Pritchard Street when I could. Even while the court was sitting, I concentrated on my SACTU duties. Helen Joseph wrote that "during the trial there were days on end when he could have heard nothing of the proceedings, for there he was, union files and cards spread out on each side of him, or on the seat of the bench in front of him, making his many entries".[16] I was greatly helped by the workers and shop stewards in the SACTU unions. They kept the faith and carried on bravely even while the Treason Trial dragged on. They did not allow anybody to take advantage of the absence of their leaders and often secured new concessions, better rules and benefits. I have no doubt that some of them played an active role in COSATU during the new democratic dispensation did so. If I did not offer my thanks and admiration appropriately at the time, I do so now in this memoir.

The intense experience in the long trial assisted me greatly and helped to develop my own people skills and respect for others. It was indeed in the cells that I observed the character, leadership and qualities of our first president of the democratic

Republic of South Africa. During the times I spent discussing matters concerning the trial, I observed the role of Nelson Mandela. He showed much concern and feeling for all the detainees, especially the young and old. He visited them in their cells, enquired about their families and asked if they had been contacted by them. He enquired if they had sufficient food, clothing, books and notepaper pads. On their behalf he would take up complaints with the prison authorities and demand appropriate conditions. He argued that the detainees were people who were not charged with offences but there in terms of a state emergency. Nelson used rules and regulations to argue for improvements and effectively established a common bond. There were many of the ANC leaders I had come to know over the years of my activities, especially among the 156 arrested on charges of treason and offences in terms of the Suppression of Communism Act and many who I believe could have become president or party leader. But I was convinced that it would be Nelson. His experience was hugely considerable and his role in the detention cells was a dress rehearsal for the subsequent Rivonia Trial and his legendary role for 27 years in Robben Island.

The Treason Trial: Contours and conclusion

Initially the prosecution in the High Court was led by Advocate Oswald Pirow, a notorious Nazi supporter of German origins – and indeed the very person whose sentiments alarmed my mother way back in September 1939. Pirow was regarded in political circles as a Fascist opportunist who in the 1930s wanted desperately to become prime minister. The prosecution of the Treason Trial was seriously flawed. It was an inept plot to create an epic trial of over 150 people who were alleged to have plotted the overthrow of the state by force and violence. Their intention – the prosecution averred – was to establish a communist state based on the Freedom Charter adopted in Kliptown. Imagine the consequences of arresting the strongly committed leaders and activists and trying them at a central place, in the Johannesburg Drill Hall. That surely was an indication of the mind and the overconfidence of the National Party government. What did Pirow or the government expect the accused to do? Offer a voiceless response to an obvious attempt to eliminate the Congress Alliance and incarcerate or hang its leadership? Did they think the accused would be so busy defending themselves that political opposition would cease? It is possible that they did not consider the consequences of their actions or care? Of course, we used the situation to plan and lead the "struggle" from the well of the court. We planned national work stoppages, boycotts and marches, and we launched national campaigns to recruit and organise workers into trade unions. In hindsight, these were years in which some of the most successful strikes, marches and trade union organisation took place. The government plot to eliminate its main opposition failed and the non-nationalist white parties succumbed to intimidation of the ruling party.

It is amazing how incompetently the Crown structured its case. Our defence counsel was quick to challenge the prosecution's argument that all the accused in this alleged conspiracy knew the grand design of this treasonous plot; and they demanded that the state prove how each of the accused was linked with this conspiracy to overthrow the state and establish a communist system. Inevitably, the legal counsel for the state had to reformulate its case and between 1956 and

1958 spent much time trying to identify relevant actions and evidence before it could get the trial up and running. It would eventually rely on the Freedom Charter as the keystone of its case – that it was a blueprint for a communist state – but this would fail. The weaknesses of the prosecution case were evident when it successively reduced the number of accused from 156 to only 30. Only if the state were successful against that group would it bring to trial those no longer "accused" but listed as "co-conspirators". Our struggle was genuinely non-violent. The prosecution, no matter how hard it tried, could not refute this fact. At the last moment, just before the state of emergency ended and our legal team returned to the courtroom, the state sneaked in a new argument. This was to the effect that the accused adopted a policy of "contingent retaliation", meaning that we adopted a policy of deliberately provoking violent retaliation by the forces of the state.

This preposterous argument was a further failure. On Wednesday, 29 March 1961 the Court rejected the prosecution's allegations and found the accused not guilty of any of the charges levelled against them. "It is impossible for this Court to come to the conclusion that the African National Congress had acquired or adopted a policy to overthrow the State by violence", concluded Presiding Judge Rumpff. It was a triumphant day for us and we were overjoyed. We moved to the front courtyard of the Old Synagogue and demonstrated our appreciation for our legal counsel. I remember Patrick Maloa (Accused no. 9 who was subsequently killed in action in Zimbabwe) help a few other well-built and strong comrades lift Isie Maisels to their shoulders and carry him from the courtroom to the courtyard. We were free; the Freedom Charter, which was at the centre of the prosecution case was no longer "on trial". It was also a victory for our families who we had comforted at the Old Fort with such composure: the charge of high treason is absurd, and we will be able to go home soon, we said – albeit it took a lot longer than our optimism predicted. Our declaration of our aims and objects for the peaceful liberation of South Africa was not a crime. I was jubilant and ascended the steps of the treason trialists' bus and sat next to Lilian Ngoyi, who was equally overjoyed. The treason trialists sang freedom songs for the last time, after so many years of travelling backwards and forwards from Johannesburg to Pretoria. Many of us must have pondered, as I did, what and where we would be in the trying days ahead. Some never met again due to exile, underground activities, bannings and arrests, which were to become a consistent occurrence.

After the trial and the immediate jubilation were over, we took advantage of the short political hiatus to celebrate the end of the long years consumed by the Treason Trial. There was much partying, which also afforded us the opportunity to thank our legal counsel, donors and helpers. I particularly recall the lively and crowded victory party in the home of Molly and Bram Fischer in the leafy suburb of Oaklands in Johannesburg. It marked the end of an important decade of my life. In August 1961 I celebrated my 32nd birthday. It was a busy and demanding time to return to full-time work. There were considerable administrative and political responsibilities to deal with in any day's work, which made it a challenging yet rewarding time. There were limited resources and we had to be innovative, finding new methods of operating, acquiring funds from sympathisers, persuading our printers to print leaflets which they feared might expose them to prosecution, deciding where to hold conferences and what to discuss at them. The ever-recurring problem was that resources were not easily available and it needed imagination to acquire them. The problems we encountered in 1961 were familiar: almost five years on, the situation was as "normal" as it had been before the upheavals of the Treason Trial, Sharpeville and detentions without trial. I resumed my full-time work as a trade unionist and as president of SACTU. It was astonishing that so much was in place after years of daily attendance at court and hasty returns to the offices in the evenings after the bus transported us back to Johannesburg.

In retrospect, in the years 1956 to 1963 we were engaged on two fronts: first in the courts, defending the threat to the existence of anti-apartheid opposition, which predominately included the Congress movement; secondly, maintaining the ongoing struggle for democratic and social justice in the townships, cities and rural areas. Looking back to that period it is also significant and important to note that there was a solid working relationship between the members of the alliance, a closeness which we, in post-apartheid years, must appreciate and replicate.

Ten
Celebrations, Detention and Exile

The number of radical activists, leaders and well-known political personalities who were served with banning orders under the terms of the Suppression of Communism Act continued to increase. The bans specifically forbade participation in political gatherings, but it was not entirely clear what was or was not a social gathering. If, however, the law had intended to outlaw social gatherings, we disregarded it, and continued to make the most of these events. We never heard of any arrests on charges of unlawful attendance at genuine social occasions. Perhaps this may have been because the powers in control had their own reasons for permitting us to meet socially: this would certainly account for the brazen behaviour of Special Branch detectives while they observed those of us who attended social events. They sat in their cars until late in the evening with the intention of intimidating us and seeing who was entering or leaving the venue. It was of course apparent that our vehicle numberplates would be noted and placed in police files with more details of the owners if they could get them.

Social occasions were increasingly less frequent as restrictions increased and many close comrades and good friends were being spirited out of the country to continue their political activities overseas or nearer home in countries such as Zambia and Tanzania. Attending parties provided a way in which like-minded people could meet and enjoy themselves – as I did. I was rather serious-minded for my years, but nevertheless enjoyed the fun of partying and mixing with friends and comrades. It was at one of such parties that I met Lorna Borkum in 1961, at the house of Ben and Mary Turok in the Johannesburg suburb of Orange Grove. It was a lively event; people were enjoying meeting friends, talking in groups, or dancing. Typical of the Turoks' functions, there were friends and activists present from all edges of the colour line. At that time, Lorna was 24 years old and after completing a degree in Psychology at the University of the Witwatersrand she had recently joined the National Union of Distributive Workers (NUDW) as a trade union organiser. She was also a member of the Congress of Democrats. I had heard about her from other members but met her for the first time at this party. We seemed to have a lot to talk about, especially her recent interesting tour to the UK and other countries in Europe. She obviously enjoyed travelling abroad and meeting thought-provoking people. She spoke about some of those whom she had met, such as Joseph Nitti, the son of former economist and Italian Socialist Prime Minister Francesco Nitti. The family was prominent in the Italian Socialist movement and had played a challenging role. Lorna also chatted about her short stay in France, which coincided with the last stages of the colonial war in Algeria, and the palpable tensions and uncertainty in Paris.

All this – and her work as a trade unionist at the NUDW: there was a lot to talk about. I recall the warm and friendly chatter of friends who left the dance floor to sit on the Turoks' verandah and were obviously relishing the evening. We decided to dance and moved to the floor, Lorna remarkably steady on her rather high-heeled shoes and looking good in her attractive clothes. She obviously felt comfortable in this crowded milieu, in which a calm friendship prevailed, and people were getting to know others whom they had not previously met. Lorna's conversation was stimulating and there was much in our minds which we were keen to discuss. I was attracted to her and suggested we meet again soon. We did and continued to see each other regularly after this first happenstance. There was, however, an interruption when I failed to turn up on a Sunday morning at her home in Illovo. She had no way of knowing where I was but was quick to suggest to Dink and Gertie Borkum, her parents, that I must have been arrested and was probably locked up in a local jail. The next morning, when the *Rand Daily Mail* was delivered, she read about my arrest on a charge of infringing the restrictions of my banning order by participating in a political gathering. I have described my arrest and detention at Marshall Square police station elsewhere in this memoir, but for the sake of this tale it is sufficient here to say that my relationship with Lorna continued despite this setback. There was much to share regarding our daily doings, politics and available cultural opportunities such as the production in September 1961 of Athol Fugard's *The Blood Knot* in which Fugard and Zakes Makae played the leading roles.

There were other house parties to which we were invited, and I recall meeting new attendees, young and angry activists who were attracted to the movement and ready to make important individual sacrifices to put an end to racial discrimination and apartheid. My relationship with Lorna deepened as we saw more of each other and shared our views and interests. We had different family histories but there was much that we found interesting to discuss in each other's lives. We had grown up in Yeoville and both started our education at the quaint primary school in Observatory, albeit with an eight-year gap between our attendance. Nevertheless, we remembered the school and some of the teaching staff and the principal, Miss Cheshire. Indeed, we were familiar with the area in which we both grew up and had some school friends and acquaintances in common; we recalled the shops, people who frequented the public swimming pool, and surrounding suburbs.

I was interested to know more about the NUDW; its leadership figures were known to be progressive and were concerned about the divisions in the trade union movement. It was a prestigious union and its reputation preceded the great contribution that incoming organisers and officials were making. Many of us, myself included, knew some of the founding organisers of the NUDW who assisted in its formation and worked there until they retired or were banned in the early 1950s. It was established initially in Cape Town in 1936 with assistance from other trade union organisers: Eli Weinberg, Ray Alexander, Katie Kagan, Pauline Podbury and Bella Page. As mentioned earlier, when I started work at Bacher Aaron in the late 1940s I joined the NUDW and later became a member of the Johannesburg branch committee. At that time Joe Slovo and Mannie Brown found jobs and participated in a long strike when the union gained many concessions from the distributive trade. I believe Lorna may have reminded them and other former trade unionists of her distinguished predecessors in the NUDW: it was already apparent that she was cut out for an important trade union career and capable of achieving success. There were trade union officials of unregistered African trade unions who needed assistance and she was becoming known as a comrade who was prepared to help grow the movement. I believe that Lorna was bound to become a significant South African trade union leader were it not for the prevailing political situation which meant that career plans were not easily attainable. She has written her own account of her union work in *Radical Engagements*, a well-received and significant memoir.

In 1962 we decided to get married and chose May Day for the event. My mother and my siblings and Lorna's parents attended the brief formal ceremony at the magistrate's office in Rissik Street. The apartheid regime's racial stance prevented any people of colour from attending the short, austere ceremony. This was as we had expected – an unhappy moment for us to be without all our comrades and friends present. But we made up for it when we celebrated that evening at our wedding party. It was an unforgettable multi-racial dance party; probably the last for many years as the political situation was now seriously challenging as a result of sterner police actions and the imminent threat of arrest under the terms of the 90-day law. The party took place at the home of Ray and Michael Harmel. We invited our family, friends and many close comrades, and by all accounts it was a memorable occasion. No photographs of the party were taken, for security reasons; but the images of many present will always be remembered by the streets, buildings and public places named in their honour soon after Nelson Mandela led his party into the new democratically elected government of national unity. Lorna and I were fortunate to be able to celebrate the sixtieth anniversary of our wedding party in Cape Town in May 2022.

Some of our guests were already quite well known to my mother, including Kathy Kathrada, Hilda and Rusty Bernstein, the Harmels, Moses Kotane, Mark Shope and other fellow trade union organisers. Winnie Mandela, who was a friend of Lorna's, was also with us. Dink Borkum, who knew a number of the guests professionally, kindly provided ample catering and a wide range of alcohol – which of course was not supposed to be served in a multi-racial setting under apartheid. There were some flattering speeches and the presentation of gifts. Michael Harmel made the first welcoming speech. I had known him and Ray since I was a teenager, and indeed lived in the "granny-flat" attached to their home for a few years before Lorna and I got married. Mark Shope and Phyllis Altmann congratulated us and presented a wedding gift on behalf of SACTU: a ceramic plate which we have admired for the past sixty years. I particularly recall the late Mosie Moolla who died at the age of 88 in March 2023. He gave us a straw picnic basket with bowls inside it. He and I had been treason trialists together and were good friends.

The party ended at midnight and we stayed at Helen Joseph's house which was not far from the Harmel home. Helen offered us her cottage while she and some other Congress Alliance members were away in the Transkei where they were establishing alternative schools, which they called cultural clubs, to offset the poor schooling provided by Bantu Education. The terms of my banning order prohibited us from leaving the magisterial area of Johannesburg, so our honeymoon was a brief holiday in the boutique Balalaika Hotel in Morningside. We then lived in Helen's cottage for some weeks, having promised to look after her formidable cat. We did so with apprehension as she was one of Helen's most prized possessions. We moved from there into our first home, a flat in Auden Court, in Berea's Olivia Road, and resumed our respective trade union and political activities.

These were uncertain days which may be described as the proverbial lull before the storm: ominous, strange. Activists clandestinely crossed over the South African borders into the then British protectorates of Swaziland, Bechuanaland and Basutoland (now eSwatini, Botswana and Lesotho after winning independence from Britain in 1966). In the meanwhile, South African police continued raids for pamphlets, incriminating documents, and general surveillance. We realised that there was more to come. Soon after we settled in our flat in Auden Court there was, not unexpectedly, a knock at our front door. As usual, two familiar faces: Special Branch detectives presented a warrant to search the premises. I cannot recall whether I asked for the reason and purpose of the raid, although I knew that they were looking for documents, banned books and magazines. I am sure that their intentions included intimidation, especially of our visitors: Bern and Jenny Janks, who were Lorna's uncle and aunt, and Molly Anderson, a close friend of ours and cousin of Bram Fischer. While the detectives were ransacking our kitchen, bedroom, cupboards, bookshelves and wardrobes, Molly indicated that she needed to use the toilet – where she wasted no time in flushing incriminating documents out of the way. After some time, the detectives left the flat, and we asked our guests if they wanted to leave. They refused to do so and stayed with us and talked. This was truly an act of solidarity which we appreciated. In the 1960s the political atmosphere in the country was changing, and one often realised that friends, relatives and neighbours avoided being seen talking to political activists for fear that they too would be watched by the Special Branch. My sister Goldie recalled, many years later, that some of her friends, including some of our relatives, crossed the street to avoid talking to her.

I continued with my SACTU activities but was careful to avoid being arrested for infringing my banning order, taking care to find safe houses where we could meet and plan. Lorna was well practised in persuading friends who were not involved with the political movement to allow us to use their homes for political meetings. In 1962 SACTU was campaigning for a national minimum wage of £1 a day. SACTU organisers stood with handwritten placards on the steps of Johannesburg's city hall and handed pamphlets to passing workers. Almost fifty years later the CCMA exhibited pictures of those events and I was surprised to see images of slogans on placards in my handwriting. The important point for us was to organise workers and recruit them into trade unions at open meetings. We took the view that trade unions would grow and be effective at open meetings. Organisers like Aaron Mahlangu, John Nkadimeng, Nimrod Sejaka, John Gaetsewe, Uriah Maleka, Mabel Balfour and Rita Ndzanga deliberately exposed themselves to persistent Special Branch surveillance, irrespective of the possible consequences. Trade unionism flourishes in meetings and demonstrations and while it was necessary at times to organise clandestinely, open meetings and events were the conditions that cemented loyalties and encouraged progress. SACTU continued to work as best it could. The Management Committee met regularly and continued to function despite security problems, which always required extra precautions and awareness.

It was at a Management Committee meeting in early 1963 that Lorna was appointed to represent SACTU at a major trade union conference in Paris in May 1963. In the scheme of Cold War political rivalries and struggle for allegiances, the conference was looked upon as of high political import. The Confederation Générale du Travail (CGT) was at that time an important centrepiece of trade union solidarity and was aligned with the World Federation of Trade Unions (WFTU). For SACTU, the WFTU offered both moral and financial support, and although we were not formally affiliated to it, there was an ideological bond. By 1960 the rapidly growing Pan-African trade union federations were being wooed both by the WFTU and the pro-west International Confederation of Free Trade Unions (ICFTU). The international trade union movement was an early victim of the Cold War and split into the two rival organisations in 1949. The Cold War in 1963 was at a crucial stage and the international trade union movements were drawn into the fray in that heightened political environment. It was important for the West and East to gain as much advantage as possible in their attempts to reach a partial international test ban treaty. This was quietly under discussion between the competing powers and by August 1963 matured into the International Test Ban Treaty.

Lorna had a South African passport, but it was only valid until May 1963 and it was considered unlikely that an application for renewal would be granted if she applied in South Africa. An obvious, and superior, strategy was for her to leave the country earlier, in March, even though the CGT conference was only due to begin on 11 May. It was an unnerving mission, which required much preparation; she had to provide plausible reasons for her failure to apply earlier while in South Africa. Nevertheless, the strategy worked and her passport was renewed when she visited the South African embassy in Trafalgar Square. In her memoir, *Radical Engagements,* Lorna relates her success in acquiring a passport, which enabled her to stay in London and use the available time before the CGT conference to speak about the role of South African trade unions and the struggle against apartheid. She spoke at a series of trade union branches and conferences in England and Scotland before travelling to Paris.

At the time, the political climate in South Africa was changing discernibly. There was a strange, grim sense of anticipation: of government inevitably closing in on its opponents; of intensive police observation as we continued our trade union and political activities; and of the Special Branch virtually on the heels of union organisers; and Congress leaders who were prepared to make themselves available to assist and to plan. Some comrades who were under unremitting pressure required alternative accommodation for a few days before they could disappear out of the county. This was not an area in which I had much expertise; I had only limited experience of assisting trade unionists who were on their way to overseas conferences and sought advice. But this was a task for the movement's specialists who were versed in taking activists to the borders of neighbouring countries and advising them on where to go and how and whom to contact. I talked to John Gaestsewe and Leslie Massina just before they escaped. It occurs to me now that there was no time for emotional farewells – just practicalities. It seemed likely to be a matter of weeks rather than months that those of us who were still in the country would be arrested.

I continued to work in the offices of SACTU, the Food and Canning and the Laundry Workers unions and made no plans to leave the country, even though I realised that arrest under the General Laws Amendment Act was imminent. The Act enabled the police to arrest and detain people for 90 days, and to release them at the end of that period, only immediately to re-arrest them for a further 90 days. The Act did not require the police to lay formal charges against their victims. Lengthy periods of detention without trial – eventually extended indefinitely – became a notorious tool for the use of torture to extract information. I was not intimidated. I lived in anticipation of what might happen and was not surprised when two Special Branch detectives arrived at our Auden Court flat on 15 May 1963 with a warrant to arrest me. The police did not enquire where Lorna was and I presumed they perhaps knew she was out of the country. (In fact Lorna was a few days into the CGT conference when she read in the London *Times* a brief piece on an inside page with news of my arrest.)

The notion of indefinite arrest without trial or charge in "normal" circumstances – as opposed to during a state of emergency as in my previous detention – was a new departure and I was not entirely sure how it would differ from past experience. What we correctly suspected was that it would eat more deeply into the already precarious legal framework of the country. Indeed, the Minister of Justice B.J. Vorster, proclaimed that he would be willing to detain people too "this side of eternity" – a sentiment that was not lost on those who became victims of this new form of incarceration. For me, arrest and detention had been a pattern of my life since December

1956: prison cells, prison food, routines and regulations, rules regarding visitors, the different attitudes of individual warders, solitary confinement and the prospect of permanent unknown harassment. I was taken to Marshall Square police station in the centre of Johannesburg and requested to hand over personal possessions such as my wristwatch, wallet, loose coins, pens or pencils, belts or braces, and any other item of concern to the superintendent or required by prison rules. Two warders escorted me to the first floor of the prison and to a cell along a corridor, leaving me there to face the foreseeable future in solitary confinement. The cell was familiar. I recognised it immediately as the same one that I had been in when I was charged with contravening my banning order. It was the same cell with the same barred dirty window. It faced the street; the mattress was covered with familiar old grey blankets. I looked around the cell and up at the window, but there was little I could see. I walked around for a while contemplating who else might have been picked up. I was one of the first to be detained under the new 90-day Act.

Whenever I was arrested and eventually put in a cell, I made up for lost sleep. Now I sat down on the mattress, which was unduly uncomfortable. I could feel something like a plank of wood underneath. I picked up the mattress and there discovered the cause of the discomfort. It was a hard-covered collection of writings by Oscar Wilde! It might have been left there by a previous awaiting trial prisoner. I settled down on the mattress and slept for what seemed like a long time. It was only mid-day, and I reminded myself that time passed slowly in solitary confinement. I looked over the Oscar Wilde stories, and turned to the long poem *The Ballad of Reading Gaol* – a very sympathetic depiction of the plight and repetitive routines of prisoners in a jail in southern England. What impressed me was his gentle observation of the prisoners walking in the prison yards and his portrayal of them as people in trouble. I put the book back in its hiding place as I heard the tinny sound of dishes in the corridor outside my cell. The door opened and a warder placed a dish of food next to me. I could hear voices and a clanging door and asked him if more people had arrived and were in the cells. He said yes, but would say no more. Later I was escorted to a prison yard which was small compared with what I was used to in the old Fort or the Pretoria Local jail. I was escorted to the statutory 30-minute exercise yard and this routine continued until the end of my stay. Ruth First, in her book *117 Days* – which she wrote after release from two continuous periods of detention in Marshall Square – referred to a remark I had written on a wall in the prison yard: Leon Levy – 90 days or eternity? She said that I added four question marks to my citation of Vorster's infamous words. I remember writing it, but cannot recall how I found the chalk or whatever it was that I used to do so.

It became apparent to me that these were early days for the 90-days system of detention and police interrogation. The Act provided for a magistrate to visit the cells, and if necessary to hear and act upon any complaints or questions. I complained to the magistrate that I had not been told why I had been arrested and demanded my release, but this was of no concern or interest to him. A Special Branch officer would sometimes appear in my cell and ask if there was anything I had to say; and I would reply sternly that I had nothing to say. He would make a note of that and leave the cell. I remained in solitary confinement, allowed out only for the usual half hour of exercise. But by now I had found out that Wolfie Kodesh, a long-standing comrade, had been arrested and was in the cell next to mine, while in a cell opposite ours were Mosie Moolla and Abdulhay Jassat. They were younger than me, and rather daring in the way that they persuaded the very young warder responsible for our section to allow me and Wolfie to talk to each other for a short while before returning to our cells.

We were indeed fortunate to be early detainees under the General Laws Amendment Act as the Special Branch had not yet started to interrogate detainees as they did a little later, using a range of forms of torture and intimidation to extract information. The use of torture appears to have increased after the arrests of the MK leadership at Rivonia in July 1964 – by which time I was no longer in detention. Our jail routine continued, and sometimes Wolfie, Mosie, Abdul and I were allowed by the young warder to talk briefly before being locked into our respective cells. It was, incidentally, the same warder – his name was Greef – who later that year assisted Mosie and Abdul, together with Arthur Goldreich and Harold Wolpe, to escape from Marshall Square. He served three years of a six-year sentence for assisting the four detainees in return for a promise of money.

Back in my cell, I often walked around it and considered the chances of release and what was in store for now and for the future. It was quite apparent that I would no longer be allowed to be actively involved in my trade union work or in the political resistance movement. I was acutely aware that in December 1962 SACTU had been listed in a government proclamation under which over 400 people were banned from holding office in any of those organisations. The names included 45 officials of

SACTU and its affiliates. My personal and political activities in South Africa were no longer possible and the prospect of exile had to be a serious consideration. Wolfie had already indicated that he was considering applying for an exit visa, which a number of other activists had been granted by the state. An exit visa was a one-way ticket to exile and was obviously an option that I had to take seriously. There was no opportunity to talk this over with Lorna or her parents and my family; but after further earnest reflection I applied for an exit visa. As Lorna wrote long afterwards, "From his little cell in detention, it must have been so strange to make such a momentous decision in isolation – to decide to leave on those absolute terms, so final, to go away, into heaven or hell".[17]

Thanks to Lorna's father, Dink, and members of my family, the exit visa, air tickets and other necessary arrangements were made after my application was granted. On 4 July 1963, I was taken by Special Branch officers to Jan Smuts Airport – now of course named after Oliver Tambo – and released from custody. It was a sad farewell for me, my family, and Dink and Gertie Borkum. And for the last time I was to say goodbye to the old stalwart Mary Levy – and hear her say, through her tears, that she was not likely to see me again. She never did. My mother died suddenly in September 1965. Lorna wrote that it was then that "I finally understood the significance of exile. It was our personal family tragedy that neither of her twin sons attended their mother's funeral." I was in London; Norman was six months into a two-and-a-half-year-long sentence in Pretoria Local Prison.[18]

Eleven
Back to the Front

It was July 1997. After 34 years in exile, Lorna and I were back in South Africa, in Cape Town. My daughter Emma and her partner Mark, and their three-year-old son, Jonny, would soon follow. A little later, on 30 September 2010, my granddaughter Daisy would be born in Cape Town. In contemplating my return from exile, it became clearer to me as the time came closer to leaving Britain that I should update my knowledge and understanding of South African custom and practice at the workplace and elsewhere. I wanted to understand the essence and nature of the fresh freedoms implemented since 1994. I wanted to know what new facts and skills had improved or hindered industrial practice during my years of exile. The trade union movement and its allies in the mass democratic movement had forced the National Party government in the 1970s to legislate important concessions, especially regarding recognition of trade unions and unfair labour practices. These were radical changes that indeed came to be an element in apartheid's retribution for its criminal acts. Most importantly, the Mandela government, almost immediately after the 1994 elections, enacted innovative new additions to in the Basic Conditions of Employment Act. It comprised equal opportunities, codes of good conduct and best labour relations practices.

Lessons from my experience in Britain

It is necessary, very briefly, to reflect upon my experiences in British industrial relations and some of the key lessons I learned through them. Before I became a practitioner, I was a student, fortunate to be studying politics, economics and industrial relations at Ruskin College in Oxford. Academic experts in industrial relations like Hugh Clegg and John Hughes were able to analyse and assess the many ideas floating about in the UK at that time. I was a student just when when labour relations were being professionally scrutinised and reconsidered. Industrial relations practices were placed under a microscope as the UK government, trade unions and employers' associations were no longer able to cope with a creaking traditional system which evolved from the time of the industrial revolution in the late 18th century. Now, two hundred years later, it required modernisation as the system rapidly fell into chaos. Strikes, lockouts and other forms of industrial action were often clashes between employers and workers over everyday arrangements that were traditional and mostly unwritten. I was told by trade unionists that hardly any formally written agreements existed. They joked that wage deals were written on the back of a packet of "fags" and that workplace customs, rules and practices were informal rather than written. And the Ruskin course included much discussion on the nature of voluntary rules and regulations. The latter are important as they are usually legislated and less flexible. Indeed, they are stricter and more formal and become collective agreements.

The theory I acquired at Ruskin soon became tested as practice. When I decided to specialise in industrial relations in the UK, especially in the oil and motor manufacturing industries, there were already experiments and extensive consultations in train. Employers, trade unions and workers were engaged in consultations, at the Esso and Mobil Oil refineries and also in the motor manufacturing factories at Ford, British Leyland and Chrysler. They were seeking more methodical ways of achieving manufacturing efficiencies and better ways of negotiating appropriate rates for jobs and systems of payment. There was a history of militant prolonged strike actions over changes in working arrangements. Workers were not prepared to accept unilateral changes to their terms and conditions.

There was not a well-developed culture of meaningful dialogue between the negotiating parties. Union officials and company labour relations executives waited for a formal meeting to take place, and this often resulted in a rapid breakdown of negotiations and consequent work stoppages or demonstrations. I tried to persuade the negotiating parties to communicate with each other before formal negotiations commenced, so that they could explain what they had in mind without compromising their positions. It was a way of avoiding tensions and disagreements. This was not the custom and they initially chose not to follow this advice. However, when negotiations broke down and the negotiating parties were at a loss at what to do, they asked me to go ahead with my approach. I did so and there was now open and sufficient dialogue which often prevented work stoppages. Hence, I was constantly arranging informal as well as official meetings with the trade unions and employer representatives.

Negotiations centred on improvements in productivity by way of looking at a job, and each of its parts required to make it. In addition, there were studies as to whether all the tasks were actually necessary, or if they could be reduced or redesigned to achieve greater efficiency. Joint involvement of the parties in these investigations was far away from the oppressive and exploitative time and motion studies of the past. There is no better expert than the person who operates a machine; he or she knows what flaws there are in a process and is able to offer suggestions for improvements. At Mobil Oil's refinery at Coryton in England, workers and plant engineers examined each task that made up a complete job and identified savings, which could be made, by taking out an unnecessary task or making changes to it. Savings were shared between the company and the workforce. Using this formula, the wage increases turned out to be higher than in the case of the previous system of negotiating on the basis of changes in the cost-of-living indices.

In the years I worked in Britain, there were far-reaching international developments. The mind-boggling idea of an integrated European Community took off into sustained growth. As the Cold War subsided, and security suspicions loosened, member states agreed to the free movement of goods, services, capital and labour. Their horizons widened to integrated social wage systems and important new benefits, relating to health, safety and housing. Most farsightedly, the potential improved for the permanent peaceful coexistence of previously hostile

European states. In Germany, worker participation through worker/employer supervisory committees turned into a highly significant innovation. More generally, the system of industrial relations turned into a "science"– an arterial system of relevant and individually tailor-made rules. There were rules for every separate entity. Over and over again, the structure of the workplace is observed and there are experiments to measure what rule fits best. The collective and individual energy in the workplace increasingly attracts social scientists (Marxist or behavioralists), economists and lawyers. While arbitration, conciliation and mediation are a distinct and essential element of labour relations, in the final analysis stability and amiable relationships depend on collective agreements: agreements over rules, processes and procedures which are fair, mutually agreed and carefully crafted. They transform industrial relations into a coherent and relevant system, always in a process of improving as new situations occur.

I was fortunate in experiencing negotiations and consultations between trade unions and employers through these years of change. Productivity bargaining in Britain has yielded significant improvements in pay and conditions of employment, especially in oil refineries and motor manufacturing industries. Mutual agreement is essential, and its importance is a matter of principle in UK trade unions. I have used these tools over my long career, especially in mediation at the Commission for Conciliation, Mediation and Arbitration (CCMA), which is described in the next chapter. The development of rules-based infrastructures highlights an important shift in terms of forms of struggle – different from what we familiarly remember from the picket lines. Indeed, collective agreements, assisted by practical legislation, create an essential organisational framework for labour and capital in a globalised setting. Events and changes move fast in the global world; what previously appeared impossible, is now settled through imaginative forms of arbitration.

Back to work

Once in Cape Town, I was eager and enthusiastic to move at a fast pace, and rented an office at Pic Bel Chambers, in Strand Street, where I researched and wrote on labour relations for Andrew Levy Employment, a large and well-established national labour relations consultancy. I had heard about Andrew Levy and his work while still in England, from a Pretoria man in the motor industry. Some months before we returned to South Africa, I telephoned Levy (although we share the same surname we are not related) from the UK, and he invited me to come and see him when I arrived in Cape Town. I did so, and we talked about my work in Britain and the role I played during the modernisation of British industrial relations in the 1970s. It was agreed that I write for some of his publications. This was the start of resuming a role in the new and ever-expanding boundaries in a society in which labour, management and the state are increasingly intertwined.

I contributed to short monthly pocket handbooks and practical guides on workplace conflict, which Andrew Levy and his consultants produced for supervisors. They embraced numerous issues such as problems of performance, issues of trust and dishonesty. They provided succinct information on legal requirements and practical ways of dealing with them.

This provided many opportunities for me to share knowledge and best practice wherever people work throughout the country. This was an innovative practical contact with the realities of the workplace, which included the observance of facts or events I wrote of initiatives to establish crêches in factories, productivity practices in mines, and many other experiences relating to important workplace issues. Each case study considered workshop practices and practical solutions to resolve problems. Some of them were much sought-after mini–Andrew Levy publications. They are now, almost certainly, part of a practitioner's library. It is, I believe, appropriate here to convey my thanks to Andrew for including me in his team.

I was planning to continue active participation in South Africa, as I had done before I was forced into exile. I wanted to share and build on the activities, skills and experience I had gained in exile. So I set about familiarising myself with new laws and institutions, which were part of the work in progress in achieving changes in the political and social formations in South Africa. Post-apartheid South Africa is now a welcome player in a globally centred world. It has access to important and relevant social, political and economic institutions in Africa and many international organisations. But it will be increasingly expected to make its own contributions to bettering international structures, which affect labour and capital. Moreover, given its considerable manufacturing and agricultural interests, and its mineral resources including coal, gold, platinum and numerous other metals, it is inevitable that South Africa will play an appropriate role in coping with climate change as it becomes an increasing threat to health, safety and employment.

I envisaged my role, as before exile, as that of an active

participant in shaping the social, political and industrial environment. Inevitably, the spheres in which I would participate related to what I knew best: namely, improving the lives and aspirations of working people. The horizons have changed, and participation in the transformation for an inclusive society essentially requires cooperative links between organised management, labour, government and a thriving civil society. This coalition of independent parts is essential to ensuring the desired strategic, economic and social direction of the country. It embraces a new generation of rights and obligations, processes and procedures, systematic and well-constructed arrangements for higher productivity and involvement in the codification of labour relations legislation and practices. Matters like these had been the subject of theoretical discussion and practical involvement during the years I lived, studied and worked in the UK. They were years of stimulating philosophical, economic and social change. There were new approaches to exploring the limits and understanding of industrial democracy, which was transforming rapidly, and included new areas of welfare and social justice.

I could not have returned to South Africa at a better time. A raft of new legislation had been passed or was in the pipeline. The Labour Relations Act – passed in 1995, two years before my return to South Africa – had values which are highly regarded as unquestionably essential to defend and nurture progressive change in the country. This was indeed a model of groundbreaking contemporary international good practice. It included a host of International Labour Organization (ILO) conventions which entrenched the ideas and principles of good faith and fairness. The legislation was rapidly followed by several specific codes of good practice. There was in addition an Employment Equity Act, intended to promote equality in the workplace and prevent unfair discrimination, relating not only to racism but other forms of exploitation, especially of women, who are paid and treated less favorably.

Earlier in 1997 the Basic Conditions of Employment Act became law. This regulated the rights and obligations of employers and employees in respect of leave pay entitlements, particulars of employment, termination, hours of work, annual leave, and other important aspects such as sectoral wage determinations. I spent the first year of my return from exile writing a step-by-step guide and analysis for users of the legislation. It was an important opportunity for me to test my understanding of factory organisation and best workplace practices – issues which I first encountered as a 24-year-old trade unionist, and later as an industrial relations specialist in the wider world. This fortuitously assisted my integration into post-apartheid South African politics and labour relations. It involved much research and contact with ministries, civil society and organisations. I met role players in politics and the labour movement who had been activists during the struggle and often detained or imprisoned during the various states of emergency declared by the apartheid government. Now many of them are civil servants or office-holders in the new dispensation.

The Basic Conditions of Employment Act is one of the high-ranking pieces of legislation, which stands with the Labour Relations Act. It regulates the requirements of employers and employees regarding rights and obligations. More importantly, they set the boundaries within which business, government and labour, can work together in creating a safe and democratic environment, guided by legislation, which encourages agreement on procedures and processes, to settle disputes, protests and the conduct of strikes. I stated in my overview of the guide:

> In the promotion and eventual passing of the new Act the Government has largely achieved what it set out to do. It has incorporated in a single Act a comprehensive range of minimum employment standards with a permissive system of flexible collective bargaining opportunities for self-regulation by employers and employees (trade unions). The hallmark of negotiated agreements must be the flexible regulation of basic conditions in line with the needs of employees for the maximum protection of employment standards and the requirements of employers for optimum operational efficiency. The government has guaranteed to millions of people in temporary, part-time or permanent employment, terms and conditions of employment which are compatible with international standards, particularly the conventions and recommendations of the International Labour Organization.

I wrote that among the most significant of these were:

> A movement to a 40-hour week and an 8-hour day; reasonable rest periods; minimum annual leave of 15 working days consecutively on full remuneration; prohibition of employment of children under 15 years of age and the protection of children who are older than 15 years from performing inappropriate work. Other international standards which the Act includes are: severance pay for loss of employment due to operational requirements (redundancy); four weeks maternity leave on full pay and protection from dismissal during a period of maternity leave; protection of health and safety of night workers, three days family responsibility leave.

The guide I wrote, "Basic Conditions of Employment", has taken its place alongside other guides on labour legislation which Andrew Levy and his consultants wrote and published. They dealt with the Labour Relations Act and issues regarding wage legislation, dismissals, absenteeism, affirmative action, retrenchment, pay, health and safety, and, most importantly the guide to the newly established Commission for Conciliation and Arbitration, the CCMA (where I would serve as a full-time commissioner for the following two decades until September 2018). The concerted effort and interest I took in understanding the new South African labour environment equipped me for a specialist role in labour relations in South Africa.

It was my good fortune to return to South Africa at a turning point in industrial relations. The role of workers, employers and government was set for urgent and radical change. Impending legislation would institutionalise relationships with firm and lasting structures for mediation, conciliation and dispute resolution. The government was publishing green and white discussion papers concerning codes of good practice on basic conditions of employment, equality at the workplace, occupational health and safety. A green paper is a broad statement of government's intended policy; a white paper seeks consultation with the public and stakeholders. It signifies a clear intention to pass a law. The language and tone of these green and white papers excited me, and serve as an indication of the new dispensation's desire to abolish the apartheid past and establish a non-racial society.

These ideals and basic human rights expressed the approval of South Africans across political parties and groupings, except of course, the minority who still favoured the doctrines of white supremacy. They are major issues of basic human rights and building blocks for generations to add to, as needs arise. Whatever malpractices and mistaken policies may occur in the future, as is often the case in revolutions, they will serve as an invisible glue to hold the democratic society together. This is what I returned to South Africa to be part of. It is the language and meaning of my core beliefs, which were written into the Freedom Charter and adopted at the Congress of the People in 1955 and are now written into the country's constitution.

Most significantly, these changes, which are designed to *revolutionise* the workplace, will represent, at the same time, a major shift, from traditional patterns of class struggle (strikes, lockouts, protests) to skilful and peaceful use of the new legislation. Shop stewards and trade union leaders will become accustomed to using the opportunities provided by the legal processes, which they created and embedded in each piece of the new legislation. Within 24 years of democratic government, there will be a shift in the traditional nature of class warfare, resulting from the trust in the new dispensation and precise ideas and clear language of labour legislation; and the willingness of the coalition of government, business and labour to actually use it. To borrow the innovative phrase of Jean and John Comaroff, sometimes the struggle will have shifted, from "warfare to lawfare".[19] Consequently, commissioners at the CCMA and judges at the Labour Courts, will experience the acquired expertise, of trade unionists, workplace managers and shop stewards. They will witness the impressive use of the legal facilities for arbitration awards and Labour Court Judgements. What would become commonplace was the sure grasp of the opportunities for concluding workable collective agreements, through professional consultation, conciliation, mediation and arbitration.

While so many of the previous danger points for strife in South Africa have now been channeled into carefully crafted paths for the settlement of disputes, this is not yet entirely the case with wage bargaining. There are now some procedural amendments, which require unions and companies to submit to a trial arbitration for an advisory award but more than this is needed. While in exile, I was involved in the negotiation of wages and changes to terms and conditions of employment. It is a branch of collective bargaining in which I could see, as did the leaders of the British trade union movement, that employer–employee participation opened up the possibility of fully involving the workforce in benefiting, from transforming operational requirements that revolutionised the workplace. Previously, this was the sole prerogative of employers. For decades they coerced employees to accept the introduction of new machinery and methods of working, leading to low rates of pay, longer working hours and inevitable job losses. Employers, irrespective of the cost of angry and consistent opposition, revolutionised their methods of production and set their standards to produce at both the most productive and profitable levels. There was not even a hint of sharing the savings from improvements which yielded greater results and could be distributed between workers and the enterprise they worked in. There was no plan to cater for employees whose job security was affected as a result of changes.

An important difference in negotiating wages and working conditions in South Africa, compared with other industrialised countries, such as the United States of America, Britain and most countries in Western Europe, is the method of consultation and negotiation of agreements for wages and working conditions. In South Africa, we tend to determine current wage movements by shifts in the cost of living. And, while intense discussions take place regarding changes in working hours and conditions, there is much emotion and less consideration of actual operational requirements which would suit workers and management.

The reason why productivity is not a feature of negotiations in South Africa is indicative of our systems of production. The cost of labour in South Africa is relatively cheap in comparison with the cost of labour in Britain. Other industrialised countries, especially in the United States of America, Britain and most countries in Western Europe, have agreed with trade union organisations and their members to participate in productivity bargaining. The result is a higher standing of living for labour and optimal levels of production for capital. In the inevitable possibility of a reduction in the numbers of the existing workforce, agreements will include safeguards against retrenchment or redundancy by way of guaranteed job security, on the basis of reduction by natural attrition.

The core value of the new South African legislation is broad worker participation, rooted in consensus-seeking consultation, wellness at the workplace, sharing the results of collective effort, new ideas on productivity to finance the shift from poverty wages to affordable rates of pay, and well-thought-through processes to generate working units to transform into profitable and sustainable enterprises. These sentiments expressed the national mood of South Africans in 1997, especially organised management and labour. As I write now in 2022, over two decades after my return from exile and extensive involvement as a commissioner at the

CCMA, this remains the political ethos. However, putting theories into practice does not necessarily always fit in with current arrangements and accumulated custom and practice. It requires mediation and arbitration and sometimes lockouts and strikes before consensus is achieved. An important lesson, which I have learned, is that change requires dedicated patience and persuasion before it can be integrated into the scheme of things.

I had returned to South Africa at a time of huge economic and structural change. I read as much as I could of the previous legislation and studied the changes proposed. There was real law in the making. And, if we fast-forward some 23 years, to 2019, the Labour Courts have risen to the challenges brought by labour, business and government. The outcomes have helped to strengthen the legislation, and pave the way for recent amendments, to improve processes and confront the task of reducing strike violence. At its centre the legislation provides for authentic democratic regulation, based firmly on the new South African Constitution and is laced with the ideals of equality and human dignity. The significance of the legislation is the skillfully embedded legal framework and lucidity, in which the legislation involves the participation and agreement of the state and organised employers and labour. What I appreciate generally is the great value of legislation, which relies on regulation by the parties involved in a dispute. The system requires them (workers, employers and trade unions) to use the legislation to facilitate, mediate and arbitrate disputes themselves. In retrospect, these structural changes have endured and thrived, despite the stresses and strains of social and economic decline, corruption and state capture, which have bedeviled development and job growth. Indeed, the quality of labour relations practice and worker participation has had the desired effect enshrined in the South African Constitution of raising the dignity of labour and the workforce.

These were issues which I worked on and implemented for three decades in Britain. Now the opportunity presented itself to use the experience and skills I had gained and to assess which international innovations would fit. In the event, this proved necessary and helpful. However, it is worth noting that many South African regulations are more explicit and legally enforceable. Moreover, in certain cases, workplace practices such as overtime work and shift changes are more amenable to adjustment than in Britain. There is, therefore, much international praise of current South African Labour legislation. In every case it has been approved, after consultation and agreement and the consent of the National Economic Development and Labour Council (NEDLAC). This is the vehicle through which government, labour and the business community consult and seek agreement.

Twelve
Taking on a New Role

Then and now: SACTU and COSATU

Eight weeks after returning to South Africa, I was invited by Mbazima Shilowa, the general secretary of Congress of South African Trade Unions (COSATU) to attend its sixth national congress in Johannesburg. It took place from the 16–19 September 1997. This was my first exposure to a South African trade union conference since I was banned in 1956 from attending all gatherings, even those of SACTU, the trade union federation of which I was the national president. My first impression was of a sea of swaying people, dressed in red T-shirts and red caps, on which were written, "An injury to one is an injury to all". I was thrilled as this had been the slogan of SACTU. Apart from this striking continuity, how different everything else seemed! In the 1950s many of the male delegates wore suits and ties and, similarly, women dressed formally and appropriately for that period. Conferences then were held in smaller halls, such as the Johannesburg Trades Hall or wherever a non-racial meeting place could be obtained. Now, it took place in the rather grand setting of the World Trade Centre in Kempton Park.

I was called to the platform and welcomed as a veteran president of SACTU – its name so similar to COSATU, with the same words in different order. I thanked the leadership and all present for their courtesy and expressed my excitement at being with them at the conference. Delegates spoke to items on the agenda with enthusiasm and urgency, but what was different was the distinct atmosphere of authority and obvious confidence in their collective identity as trade unionists. There was an acute perception of formidable power and prestige, as members of the Congress Alliance, with a role in determining the political, social and economic future of the country.

I listened carefully to Congress discussions on changes in remuneration, working conditions and social benefits such as housing, health and availability of jobs – especially for farm workers and their aspirations for land. COSATU had clearly deepened its relationship with the movement for national liberation and had established itself as a strong ally for change in South Africa. From its early roots in SACTU, organised labour had formally become a close ally of the government of the country. COSATU rose to the occasion in transforming its infrastructure in the new dispensation. It had lived up to the vision of the militant and far-sighted progressive registered and unregistered trade unions and their leaders' enthusiasm for an active role in labour relations was heightened by the developments that had taken place since 1994 and the significant new laws and structures which had been put in place.

I was particularly interested to hear speeches and discussions on international themes and was struck by the continuity in political orientation from that of SACTU in the 1950s and early 1960s. There were now more specific discussions on the economy and the necessity for a developmental state. The emphasis was on equal distribution of services and economic opportunities. There was much reference to the class struggle and consolidation of the national liberation movement's economic and social perspectives. The World Federation of Trade Unions (WFTU) was a significant pillar of South African trade union international interest during my years in the trade union movement. It was created in 1945 as a single structure for trade unions world-wide. At that time, the hope and fervour for change and peace was of overwhelming concern. All trade unions, the world over, including the British Trade Union Council and the American Federation of Labor and Congress of Industrial Organisations, were affiliated to it. Sadly, the Cold War and the division of the world into two regional blocs impacted on the labour movement. In 1950, the trade unions in the Western Bloc except the French and Italian federations) withdrew and established the International Confederation of Free Trade Unions (ICFTU). COSATU, however, broadened its international links by liaising with both ICFTU and the WFTU. COSATU was continuing the precedent of SACTU in developing links with international trade union movements.

Over the years, especially after its re-emergence in the 1970s, South Africa's trade union movement created guidelines for good leadership and its authority was firmly based on consultation with members and elected shop stewards. It derived authority through grass-root consultation. Its leaders do not have carte blanche authority to commit to changes without discussion and consent of the membership. I was impressed with this and came to appreciate its significance even more when I mediated disputes in my subsequent role as a CCMA commissioner. Consent of members and shop stewards is mandatory for settlements of disputes or agreements. In those unions where this code of conduct is not followed, the evidence of damage is seen in the proliferation of what had been a single entity into as much as five competing trade unions in the same industry.

Arguably, this was the trade union movement's finest hour. The sixth national congress in September 1997 confirmed COSATU's role in the new dispensation. This was a legendary leap into the future role that the trade union movement (all trade unions irrespective of affiliation) would play in crafting a vibrant and rules-based industrial society. What was happening now was that power relationships were changing and would challenge inequality and the social and economic status quo – the obscenities of apartheid society. Trade union shop stewards and leaders were negotiating terms and conditions with government and employers in NEDLAC, which has been established in 1994. At enterprises with more than 50 employees, statutory joint equity committees were established to monitor the fair demographic composition of the workforce. Negotiated agreements shifted the turbulent days of the struggle for national liberation to other ways and means of class struggle. These were negotiation, mediation and, as a last resort, strike action as defined and protected by the rules in the Labour Relations Act. It was at the COSATU congress in 1997 I decided that I should attempt to bring home the skills and knowledge I had acquired, including processes, procedures and innovative ideas that were not already part of South African expertise.

My career and interest in social justice in a constitutional democracy is based on the extent of participation that society enjoys. This is what drew me into active political involvement in the first place and my life's struggle for liberty for all is about that. Now there was scope for me to offer labour relations expertise. I had practical and theoretical experience in the numerous ways trade unions, government and business regulate labour relationships. I had come to understand and support rules-based industrial relations, which prevent chronic disorder and create industrial stability. Rules-based industrial relations has the effect of shaping and innovating fair social justice and good conduct. I was encouraged by the basic groundwork and single-mindedness of the South African trade union movement as I encountered it in the 1990s. It removed workplace obstacles to improved conditions, practices and remuneration structures. It says a lot for the initiative South Africans had contributed so skillfully over time. I was determined to pass on 50 years' experience to where it belonged.

There was one other way, in which I was involved, where the histories of SACTU and COSATU intersected. This was at a hearing of the Truth and Reconciliation Commission (TRC), at the Carlton Hotel in Johannesburg. The purpose of the hearing was to consider the role of business in the system of apartheid and the record of these hearings is in the official TRC report. I was part of COSATU's team and provided evidence to the TRC on the impact of apartheid on trade unions affiliated to SACTU. The evidence included SACTU's role in opposing the government's policy in 1956, which was to break organised unions by enacting the Natives Settlement of Disputes Act. The Act permitted African workers to establish factory committees in their work places but explicitly excluded any involvement of a trade union official or representative. It is to the credit of workers, throughout the country, who instinctively refused to respond to employer invitations to establish what would eventually result in a potential "sweet heart" entity. Incidentally, the notion of factory committees which exclude trade unionists remains totally unacceptable, even in the post-apartheid era.

Twenty years of arbitration and mediation

After attending the COSATU congress, I decided that the next stage of my labour relations vocation would embrace all partners: labour, business, government and community. I prepared myself for such a role in the following two years with part-time work for the Independent Mediation Service of South Africa (IMSSA). This was a prominent, progressive and well-run national industrial relations centre, which offered services that included mediation and arbitration. In the apartheid period it enjoyed the trust of employers and employees and played a major role in helping to resolve labour relations disputes, entirely independent of the state machinery. IMSSA will always be remembered for the help of respected members of the legal fraternity, such as Charles Nupen, its executive director for a decade, and other legal giants like Ismail Mahomed, Arthur Chaskalson and their colleagues in the renowned Legal Resources Centre. A number of IMSSA panellists have in the post-apartheid era gone on to become judges in the Constitutional Court, the Supreme Court of Appeal, the High Court and the Labour Court.

In my work for IMSSA I was involved in a number of disputes between schools administered by the Western Cape education department and teachers or trade unions. There were frequent disputes concerning the placement of teachers. Some parents, who served on school governing bodies, would frequently allege issues of favouritism or nepotism regarding the selection of teachers. There were also conciliation meetings concerning consistent teacher absence from the classroom or alcohol-related issues. IMSSA was prominent in industrial disputes, but I participated in only a few before I moved to the CCMA. I well remember one case in which I was involved which struck me forcibly at the time. I was allocated a conciliation case regarding a dispute between a large enterprise and the established trade unions. The matter was about terms and conditions of employment. There were a good number of employer and employee representatives present as was often the case in disputes of this sort. However, what for me was a novel experience was the array of lap-top computers on the negotiating table in front of the union officials who in this case were Africans. They took notes or referred to texts regarding previous commitments and so on. This sophistication was so different from the style of meetings in the era when I worked in the trade union movement before going into exile that I found it a moving experience.

In 1999, thanks to a generous recommendation by Mbazima Shilowa, I was accepted as a full-time commissioner at the newly established Commission for Conciliation, Mediation and Arbitration (CCMA). This was my opportunity to straddle the whole industrial relations kaleidoscope. As I have indicated, once back in South Africa it was my intention to return to active participation in the area of activity which was of paramount importance to me. I wanted to "hit the ground running" and thanks to so many colleagues, trade union officials and the leadership of the CCMA, I did just that. I began work as a CCMA commissioner three days after celebrating my 70th birthday in August 1999 and continued in my post until I reached the age of 89. My contract was renewed five times between the years 1999 and 2018 and I am taking the opportunity now to thank the Commission and all my colleagues for their support and interest in my approach and my work in mediation, facilitation and conciliation.

The CCMA has won the confidence and trust of trade unions, shop stewards and workers throughout the country. Equally so, employers in small and large enterprises throughout South Africa have come to respect its impartiality and are content to seek its assistance and procedural guidance, especially in matters concerning retrenchment of managers and well-placed staff in so many workplaces. The new political dispensation channeled disputes into the CCMA for peaceful resolution of all types of cases: discrimination, trade union recognition, interpretation of agreements, and especially processes and procedures for retrenchments. Employers, trade unions, shop stewards and workers achieved remarkable results in the management of retrenchments and redundancies. They saved jobs by examining possibilities in respect of each situation and agreed to redesign them when necessary.

For me, the following two decades passed swiftly, each year different from the last. The reputation of the CCMA grew quickly and widely in all nine provinces and had the effect of increasing our daily caseload and our individual and collective skills. Trade unions and employers soon experienced the different approaches of individual commissioners, and we became known for our skills and range of collective and individual expertise. Trade unionists and employer representatives had their own distinctiveness; and we, like them, shaped our mediating styles accordingly. Matters concerning collective agreements and alleged unfair practices predominated. Most referrals of unfair dismissal were about workplace disputes. The old practice, of apartheid times, when workplace managers shouted "pack your things and go" was no more. More often than not, in those days, victims were followed out of the workplace by fellow workers and were arrested and charged for striking illegally. Now they have the right to argue their cases before commissioners at the CCMA or bargaining councils.

In 2002, the Labour Relations Act was amended to include specific processes and procedures in the event of retrenchment and redundancy due operational requirements. This included a 60-day consultation period and a minimum of four formal meetings, and as many side meetings as necessary. A most significant feature was a mandatory requirement for parties to develop a culture of consensus seeking. This opened opportunities for widespread and genuine consultation actually involving all the people who would be affected by a change in operational requirements. Meetings became an essential vehicle to save jobs and enterprises. Today, an immensely important feature of South African industrial relations legislation is the statutory requirement for parties to a dispute to negotiate and agree picketing rules. These rules must guide industrial action from the time it commences until a settlement is agreed. Our job as commissioners was to help parties to create rules where they were needed. If the parties fail to agree to a set of picketing rules, an accredited CCMA commissioner must establish them.

Fixing such rules required experience and the confidence of the parties in the impartiality of the commissioner. This was an area of activity of special concern to me and I spent much time while with the CCMA perfecting the efficacy of rules which I helped to establish. The rules were necessarily detailed. They listed the names and telephone numbers of shop stewards, marshals and management representatives so they could be contacted at any time. They set limits to when picketing might take place and where pickets might stand or sit in order to allow vehicles to move through agreed main gates and entrances; an agreed number of pickets could exercise their right to talk to people to explain the reason for the strike and seek support. An important issue was a strike rule which specifically excluded the use of traditional weapons such as knobkerries. Many other features could be included in a picketing agreement, and they were tailor-made to suit the circumstances. If police required information regarding the legal status of a strike the parties would present a copy of the agreement and a certificate signed by the presiding commissioner. In certain cases, I persuaded parties to the agreement to meet at the end of a week if the strike was not settled in order to talk about the possibility of a settlement. This provision was designed to avoid any sign of weakening of the resolve of the parties.

To give a sense of the work involved as a commissioner, here are some illustrations of cases regarding different issues which I conciliated. There was a lengthy and complicated dispute between Cape Town City Council and the South African Municipal Workers Union (SAMWU). The City Council employed 29,000 municipal workers, most of whom were members of SAMWU, a union known for its militancy. Other workers belonged to the Independent Municipal and Allied Trade Union (IMATU).

The Council sought to reduce the numbers of the workforce and to redesign many of the jobs. Under Section 189(a) of the Labour Relations Act employers seeking to make retrenchments of changes in the conditions of employment have to meet a fairly stringent set of requirements, which – as in this case – frequently required conciliation and mediation. As commissioner, one needed to explain the process patiently and in detail. I observed that participating members of SAMWU were particularly vigilant when their union officials negotiated changes in job designs. The process of mediating between SAMWU and the Council ran for two years.

I was involved a number of times in conciliation hearings involving disputes between staff and management at the former prison on Robben Island, which is now a museum. Industrial relations on the Island were rancorous and hostile, affecting the ability of the museum to operate effectively. Conciliation was eventually achieved but it was hard won. I also handled wage disputes between the Western Province Rugby Union and their players; several issues between the University of Cape Town and its staff, ranging from grievances of the canteen workers to a clash between academics and the university over pensions. And over the 20 years, there were many, many others. Some cases were complicated, particularly when there were referrals regarding allegations of sexual harassment: male employees complaining of sexual misconduct by female supervisors, or female employees' allegations regarding unwanted sexual attention from male staff members. Evidence proffered was often long and convoluted and mixed with allegations or veiled innuendos of poor work performance or intricate other unfamiliar relationships. The substance of referrals of alleged sexual harassment, was diverse and evidence presented was sometimes sad. There were some straightforward cases of proven misbehavior, but others needed the wisdom of Solomon to fathom a fair outcome. Nevertheless, our decisions were only sometimes contested in the Labour Court.

When the government amended the Labour Relations Act, my experience in navigating retrenchment and redundancy agreements proved useful and helped to establish the Commission's interventions as fair and practicable. I counselled participating parties on the idea and use of rule-based labour relations laws. It is their skillful application which assists parties resolve their disagreements. Over time, as the CCMA was seen as a uniquely fair opportunity to resolve disputes, confidence grew, and the CCMA was embraced by trade unions and business. Mostly, as time moved on, organised labour resolved their disputes referred to the CCMA, without always resorting to industrial action. Indeed, it is common practice now, for trade union officials and shop stewards, to teach labour law-based rules at union training sessions and, at times, offer management imaginative new ideas. It is so too with business enterprises. They use the services of labour relations experts to represent them at the CCMA and labour courts. Archives and records will show how parties engaged in a dispute became innovative and often found solutions and avoided the need to refer a dispute to bargaining councils or the CCMA. The raft of labour legislation – and hands-on ideas established the basis for a stable and well-constructed system of industrial relations which is now part and parcel of everyday practice and custom throughout South Africa. A recent South African innovation is the creation of useful advisory awards by a panel of CCMA arbitrators. They aim to give the parties a chance to rethink their position with the aid of the award and create more opportunities for peaceful resolution of problems.

I was fortunate to be able to bring to the CCMA my skills and overseas experience in addition to my past as a trade union leader. I felt that I was participating in the creation of a modern industrial and social democracy. I am grateful to have played a part as a commissioner in applying the new processes and procedures, to settle disputes peacefully and to the satisfaction of the parties. In the initial years at the CCMA, I was responsible for organising teams of commissioners who successively won certificated awards for settling disputes in the Western Cape region. In 2005 I received a handsome trophy for being acknowledged as the best performing commissioner for that year in the CCMA. I felt honoured to receive a CCMA Director's Award from the then Director, Nerine Kahn, for lifetime achievement. I have many fine recollections of innovations and practices, which proved so very successful.

I had one other experience during these years that I would like to mention. After I had settled into my role as commissioner at the CCMA, I resumed my interest in peace and development on the African continent and accepted an invitation to serve on the board of the well-known and long-standing Centre for Conflict Resolution (CCR). Laurie Nathan was the director and had developed the organisation successfully into a respected local dispute resolution service. It was based in Cape Town and engaged in the resolution of disputes at workplaces, taxi associations and in communities. Considering the outcome of our democratic dispensation and new progressive legislation, the CCR board decided to establish a different role for the CCR as a centre for peace building in Africa and a "think tank" for new policies and development. Prior to moving on to these new arenas, Laurie and the board sought and appointed an experienced practitioner, Adeke Adebajo. He had considerable knowledge and hands-on experience of United Nations strategies in peace-keeping programmes and had established close ties with appropriate UN and other peace-keeping resources for funding and training policies.

This was a major change in direction, but the CCR gained knowledge and traction by selecting additional members to the board. These included the senior Ghanaian politician Mary Chinery-Hesse; James Jonah, a wise and experienced Sierra Leonean scholar with considerable UN institutional knowledge of international relations and diplomacy; and Adebayo Adedeji, a Nigerian role player known for promoting Pan-African regionalism. Also included were distinguished South Africans like Yasmin Sooka, Executive Director for the Foundation for Human Rights in South Africa; Jody Kollapen, who is now a judge of the Constitutional Court of South Africa; and Chris Landsberg who writes widely on international affairs and is Professor of African Foreign Policy and Diplomacy at the University of Johannesburg. This was a well-mixed range of distinguished and interested people whose experience we needed to engage with peace work in Africa. After serving as a member of the board for a year, I accepted election as its chairperson. In this capacity, I regarded it essential to maintain regular and well-prepared monthly meetings and of particular importance (after administrative and financial reports had been dealt with appropriately) I would invite CCR team leaders to explain to board members their role and activities in peace building in Africa.

The CCR practitioners, who had considerable experience and knowledge of Africa, worked with their counterparts "on the ground", especially in selected areas. This was always on the invitation of the local peace builders and their leaders. These missions in training and peace-keeping techniques were based on current and local practical needs and indeed home-grown interventions, which were important and often successful. They took place in African states such as the Democratic Republic of the Congo, Liberia, Burundi, Ghana, Uganda, South Sudan, Morocco and Tunisia. The CCR also engaged in peace-building interventions in countries nearer to home, in eSwatini, Lesotho and Zimbabwe. The director and staff of the Centre worked tirelessly in presenting policy documents and were much admired for their efforts in organising all-African conferences and events. Its publications were productive and served as a significant contribution to peaceful negotiation and agreements on peace issues in Africa. Chairing this board was an important addition to my life experiences. It was a voluntary contribution and capped my life-long interest in world peace, described in earlier chapters. I served on the board for almost 12 years and encouraged innovation and more local participation, involving lecturers and students from the University of Cape Town and elsewhere to attend a monthly discussion group with invited speakers.

I WAS 25 YEARS old when SACTU's Declaration of Principles was adopted in March 1955. It invoked "the spirit of brotherhood and solidarity of all workers" and unreservedly rejected "any attempts to sow disunity among the workers, on the basis of colour or nationality or any other basis". It called on the working class and other progressive-minded sections of the community to "build a happy life for all South Africans, a life free from unemployment, insecurity and poverty, free from racial hatred and oppression, a life of vast opportunities for all people". Three months later, those of us gathered at Kliptown endorsed the ideals spelled out in the ten ringing clauses of the Freedom Charter. Notwithstanding new experiences and exposure to different approaches and new ideas, I still, at the age of 93, aspire to these lofty ideals. At that time, I admit, I perhaps conflated aspiration and achievement. But to me, to aspire to those ideals remains an important goal: perhaps – like gradually attaining the ideal state of Plato's Republic – we can approximate to them and achieve significant gains, slowly, over generations.

Notes

1. L. Levy, *Radical Engagements* (Jacana Media, 2009), p. 96.
2. *Ibid.*, p. 129.
3. N. Levy, *The Final Prize: My life in the anti-apartheid struggle* (Cape Town, South African History Online, 2011), p. 18.
4. M. Shain, *The Roots of Antisemitism in South Africa* (Johannesburg: Witwatersrand University Press, 1994), pp. 12, 19.
5. M. Rubin, "The Jewish Community of Johannesburg, 1886–1939: Landscapes of Reality and Imagination," MA thesis, University of Pretoria, 2005, pp. 128, 154.
6. G. Shimoni, *Community and Conscience: The Jews in Apartheid South Africa* (Hanover and London: University Press of New England, 2003, p. 90.
7. *Ibid.*, p. 91.
8. *Ibid.*, p. 82.
9. H. Arendt, *Eichmann in Jerusalem: A Report on the Banality of Evil* (New York: Penguin, 1994), p. 273.
10. Quoted in K. Luckhardt and B. Wall, *Organize or Starve: The History of the South African Congress of Trade Unions* (London, Lawrence and Wishart, 1980), p. 91.
11. The Local Committees are described in the following chapter.
12. L. Levy, "African Trade unionism in South Africa", *Africa South in*

Exile, vol. 5, no. 3 (1965), pp. 32–43.
13 H. Joseph, *If This Be Treason* (London: Andre Deutsch, 1963) and *Side by Side: The Autobiography of Helen Joseph* (London: Zed Books, 1986).
14 Joseph, *If This be Treason*, p. 87.
15 Joseph, *If This be Treason*, p. 153.
16 *Ibid.*
17 Levy, *Radical Engagements*, p. 83.
18 *Ibid.*, p. 100.
19 J. and J.L. Comaroff, *Law and Disorder in the Postcolony* (Chicago: University of Chicago Press, 2006), p. 30.

Index

A
African National Congress (ANC) 55, 118, 119, 135, 162, 163, 169, 175
Afrikaner nationalism 24–5, 34
Alexander, Ray (also Ray Alexander Simons) 79, 80–84, 128, 137, 138, 182; *see also* Simons, Ray
Altmann, Phyllis 131, 142, 184
Andrews, Bill 56, 80, 82
ani-semitism *see* Jews in South Africa
apartheid 57, 75–6, 116
Arenstein, Bernie 59–60, 62
Arenstein, Molly 62

B
Bacher Aaron 48–9
Balfour, Mabel 101–2, 186
Bandung Conference 66
Basic Conditions of Employment Act 196, 203–4
Bernstein, Hilda 61, 64, 65, 184; *see also* Watts, Hilda
Bernstein, Rusty 54–5, 121, 122, 184
Beyleveld, Piet 111, 115, 119
Bizos, George 26–7
Borkum, Dink 134, 181, 184, 193
Borkum, Gertie 181, 193
Borkum, Lorna 180–83; *see also* Levy, Lorna
Borokhov, Dov Ber 42; *see also* Zionism
British empire 24, 145, 146
Brown, Mannie 53, 59, 182
Bunting, Brian 64, 142
Bunting, Sonia 65

C
Centre for Conflict Resolution 223–25

Coe, Gus 79, 84
Cold War 31–2, 62–3, 66, 145, 187, 213
Commission for Conciliation, Mediation and Arbitration (CCMA) 4, 5, 99, 104, 186, 199, 214, 217–23; and trade unions 218–20; issues handled by 220–22.
Communist Party of South Africa (CPSA) 2, 21, 32, 43, 52–4, 55, 59, 72, 81; *see also* South African Communist Party; Suppression of Communism Act
Congress Alliance 55–6, 77, 118, 120, 123, 124–5, 150, 174, 184, 212; and Defiance Campaign 58, 77, 163; and Congress of the People 119–23, 136; and Freedom Charter 2, 66, 121–3, 136, 206; and National Minimum Wage campaign 77, 136; and SACTU 118–9, 124–5, 135–8
Congress of Democrats 56, 118, 135, 180
Congress of Industrial Organizations (CIO) 147–50
Congress of Non-European Trade Unions (CNETU) 84, 112, 128, 129
Congress of South African Trade Unions (COSATU) 4, 46, 96, 130, 211; National Conference (1997) 211–14; and SACTU 211–16
Crawford, Archie 56

D
Dadoo, Yusuf 58, 64, 135
Damons, Stella, 74, 77, 110, 115, 130
Defiance Campaign, *see* Congress Alliance
Discussion Club 59–62
Dlamini Steven 74, 137
Du Plessis, Danie 53–4
Du Toit, Bettie 73, 79, 84, 92–3, 96

F
Federation of South African Women (FEDSAW) 136–7
First, Ruth 53, 64, 65, 68, 75, 76, 145, 191
Fischer, Bram 64, 121, 160, 167, 176, 185
Fischer, Molly 68, 176
Freedom Charter, *see* Congress Alliance

G
Goldreich, Arthur 61, 192
Goldstein, Ann 19
Guardian (British newspaper) 4
Guardian (Communist Party of South Africa newspaper) 53, 67, 81

Gummed Tapes 49–51, 61, 71

H

Habonim 13, 40
Harmel, Michael 54, 64, 183, 184
Harmel, Ray 183, 184
Hashomer Hatza'ir 40–3, 44
Hirson, Baruch 40, 43
Hodgson, Rica 55

I

Independent Mediation Service of South Africa (IMMSA) 216–17
Industrial Conciliation Act (1936) 83, 94
Industrial Conciliation Act (1956) 82–3, 107
Industrial relations in UK 5, 196–9; in South Africa 201–10
International Confederation of Free Trade Unions (ICFTU) 130, 187

J

Jason, Christina (Chrissie) 74, 77, 110, 117, 130
Jassat, Abdulhay 65, 192
Jews in South Africa, 13–14, 37–9, 40; anti-semitism 34–5, 38; and politicisation, 40, 44–5; Jewish Workers Club 38; Yididish Cultural Federation 17, 38–9; *see also* Levy, Leon
Joseph, Helen 64, 65, 66, 68, 122, 135, 137, 145, 156, 161, 162, 165, 166, 169–70, 184–5

K

Kathrada, Ahmed ('Kathy') 58, 121, 161, 162, 184
Kotane, Moses 53, 130, 137, 184

L

Labour Relations Act 202, 203, 219, 222
Lan, Rebecca ('Becky') 74, 110, 145
Levy, Andrew 200–01
Levy, David 8–9, 10, 20, 21, 24
Levy, Goldie 8, 9, 10, 13, 18, 20, 21, 24, 159–60, 86
Levy, Leon 1–224; and memoirs 1–5; parents 8; childhood and family life 7–21; schooling 23–7; books and reading 27–33, 49, 190–1; Jewish background and identity 20, 37–45; and employment after school 47–51; and Communist Party of South Africa 2, 52–4; and South African Communist Party 54–5; and Discussion Club 59–62; and Peace Council 62–8, 169–70; as trade unionist 71–2, 78–84, 86–7, 89–102, 104–106,

109–110; and SACTU 2, 3, 56, 74, 75, 111–49, 172, 177, 186–7, 189, 192, 211–13; and Congress of the People 119–23; and Freedom Charter 121–4; banning orders (under Suppression of Communism Act) 133–4, 143, 181, 184, 186, 190; and treason trial 151–77; prison and detention: in Marshall Square 133–4 (charged with breaking banning order), in Johannesburg Fort, 152–6, in Pretoria Local (detained during State of Emergency) 165–9, in Marshall Square (detained under 90-day law) 190–4; marriage and wedding party 183–4; decision to go into exile 192–3; return from exile, 3–4, 96, 195; work with Andrew Levy 200–01, 204–05; and COSATU 211–14, 215; and IMSSA 216–17; and CCMA 217–223; and Centre for Conflict Resolution

Levy, Lorna 3, 4, 5, 183–5, 187–9, 193, 195; and *Radical Engagements* 4, 183, 188; *see also* Borkum, Lorna

Levy, Mark 4–5, 9–10, 38

Levy, Mary 4, 8, 9, 12–3, 23–4, 134, 151, 159–60, 165, 193; interests, 10, 27–9; enterprises 14–21

Levy, Norman 7. 8. 9. 10. 11. 16, 18, 34, 40, 58, 151, 152, 158, 193

Lithuania 8, 14, 28, 37; *see also* Jews in South Africa

Luthuli, Albert 119, 137, 166–67

M

Macmillan, Harold 146

Maisels, Israel ('Isie') 160, 168, 175

Mandela, Nelson 4. 27, 33,76, 161, 162, 169, 170, 173, 183

Mandela, Winnie 184

Marks, J.B. 79, 84, 130, 132, 149

Marx, Karl 31–2

Massina, Leslie 61, 68, 91–2, 95, 110, 111, 115, 120, 135, 161

Mateman, Don 74, 110, 111

Matomela, Florence 77

Mbeki, Govan 76–7, 138

Mbeki, Thabo 33,77, 89

Mlangeni, Andrew 68

Moemakoe, Isaac 84, 128

Moodley, Mary 103

Moolla, Moosa ('Mosie') 58, 161, 184

Motsoaledi, Elias 68

Mpetha, Oscar 130, 145

Muller, Mike 79, 84, 130

N

Nair, Billy 74–5, 137, 149
Nathan, Laurie 223–4
National Party 1, 34, 35, 44, 160, 174; *see also* apartheid
National Union of Distributive Workers (NUDW) 49, 180, 182–3
National Union of Laundering, Cleaning and Dyeing Workers (NULCDWU) 71, 73, 128, 131
Native Labour Settlement of Disputes Act 83, 216
Ndzanga, Lawrence 89, 101, 149
Ndzanga, Rita 89, 186
New Age 75, 76, 81, 142
Ngotyana, Greenwood 74, 121, 130
Ngoyi, Lilian 137, 153, 161, 162, 166, 176
Nkadimeng, John 74, 111, 115, 149, 161, 186
Nkrumah, Kwame 67, 145
Nokwe, Duma 146, 161, 162, 168, 169

O

Ossewa Brandwag 34, 44

P

Pan Africanist Congress 67, 162, 169
Pan-Africanism 67, 145
Pirow, Oswald 39, 173, 174
Police 56, 73, 132, 133, 139–40; *see also* Special Branch
Press, Ronnie 15, 60, 74, 115, 159

R

Ruskin College 5, 33, 196–7

S

Sachs, Albie 145
SACTU *see* South African Congress of Trade Unions
Salie, Saleem 65
see also Levy, Leon
Sejaka, Nimrod 74, 149, 186
Sharpeville shootings 162–3
Shilowa, Mbazima 211, 217
Shope, Mark 95, 110, 184
Sibande, Cleopas 111
Sibande, Gert 75, 149, 161
Sibeko, Archie 74, 110, 121
Simons, Jack 83, 130
Sisulu, Walter 61, 76, 121, 135, 161
Slovo, Joe 32, 43, 54, 106, 134, 182
Sobukwe, Robert 67
South African Coloured People's Organisation 56, 118, 135
South African Communist Party (SACP) 4, 43, 55, 58, 151–2, 163, 164
South African Congress of Trade Unions (SACTU) 2, 3, 56, 74, 107–49,

161, 172, 186–7; origins 108–112; inaugural conference and constitution 112–15, 226; National Executive Committee 115, 129; combines workers' interests and national liberation 116–18, 124, 135–6; and Congress Alliance 118–9, 124–5, 135–8; local committees 130–1; Management Committee 129, 148, 186–7; activities and growth 138–44; international links and lessons 144–9; and COSATU 211–16
South African Indian Congress 118, 119, 135
South African Peace Council 61, 62, 64–8, 122, 169–70
South African Trades and Labour Council (SAT&LC) 85, 87, 107–11, 113, 127
Special Branch 56, 81, 122, 151, 164–5, 179–80, 185, 188, 189, 191, 192; *see also* police
State of Emergency (1960) 162–3

T
Thompson, Douglas 64, 65
Tloome, Dan 79, 84, 130, 149
Trade unions in South Africa 71–87, 89–106; generational shift 71–3; record-keeping 72–3, 79, 84–5; and Suppression of Communism Act 72–3, 79, 84–5; Industrial Council, 95–7; disputes 103–05; in Britain 5, 196–9; in the USA 147–50; *see also* specific trade unions and confederations
Transvaal Food Canning and Allied Workers Union 81, 90
Transvaal Indian Congress 55, 58
Treason Trial 2, 77, 115, 137, 140, 151–77; details of those accused 152–3; preparatory examination (in Drill Hall) 157–61; trial proper (in Old Synagogue) 161–2, 168–70, 173–5; accused defend themselves 168–70; trial 'as classroom' 171–3; state prosecution 173–6; verdict 176
Turok, Ben 74, 121, 180
Turok, Mary 74, 180

U
Umkontho we Sizwe 163–4

W
Watts, Hilda 39, 54; *see also* Bernstein, Hilda
Weinberg, Eli 72–3, 79, 128, 130, 157

Williams, Cecil 55
Wolfson, Issy 72, 79, 84, 128
Wolfson, Julia 84
Wolpe, Harold 53, 64, 65, 192
Workers Unity 129, 130, 144, 157
World Federation of Trade Unions (WFTU) 129–30, 187, 213

World War II 17, 21, 34–5, 44

Y
Yiddish Cultural Federation 17, 38–9
Yiddish literature 28–9, 38

Z
Zionism 40, 42–3; *see also* Hashomer Hatz'air